COMMANDER
IN
CHEAT

COMMANDER IN CHEAT

HOW GOLF EXPLAINS TRUMP

RICK REILLY

hachette
BOOKS

NEW YORK · BOSTON

Copyright © 2019 by Rick Reilly

Jacket design by Carlos Esparza

Jacket photograph © Ian MacNicol/Getty Images

Jacket copyright © 2019 by Hachette Book Group, Inc.

Hachette Books
Hachette Book Group
1290 Avenue of the Americas
New York, NY 10104
hachettebookgroup.com
twitter.com/hachettebooks

First Edition: April 2019

Hachette Books is a division of Hachette Book Group, Inc.

The Hachette Books name and logo are trademarks of Hachette Book Group, Inc.

The publisher is not responsible for websites (or their content) that are not owned by the publisher.

The Hachette Speakers Bureau provides a wide range of authors for speaking events. To find out more, go to www.hachettespeakersbureau.com or call (866) 376-6591.

Library of Congress Control Number: 2018962481

ISBNs: 978-0-316-52808-5 (hardcover), 978-0-316-52784-2 (ebook)

Printed in the United States of America

LSC-C

10 9 8 7 6 5 4

This book is dedicated to the truth. It's still a thing.

Contents

1

THE BIG LIE

To find a man's true character, play golf with him.
—P. G. WODEHOUSE

IN THE 30 YEARS I've known Donald Trump, I never believed anything he said, but the *wink-wink* of it was that I never thought he believed any of it either. He was like your crazy uncle at Thanksgiving who sits in the living room telling the kids whoppers about punching Sinatra while the parents all roll their eyes in the kitchen. He was a fun, full-of-it fabulist.

One time, for instance, I was in his office in Trump Tower. He pulled a yellow laminated card out of his wallet and slapped it down on his massive desk like a fourth ace.

"Look at that!" he said. "Only nine people in the world have that!"

The card read: *Bearer Eats Free at Any McDonald's Worldwide.*

"It's only me, Mother Teresa, and Michael Jordan!" he crowed.

I pictured Mother Teresa, at that very moment, pulling into the drive-thru at the Calcutta McDonald's, rolling down the window, leaning her habit out, and saying, "I need 10,000 double cheeseburgers, please."

I liked Trump the way I liked Batman. He was what eight-year-old me thought a gazillionaire *should* be like—his name in 10-foot-high letters on skyscrapers and on giant jets, hot and cold running blondes hanging on each arm, $1,000 bills sticking out of his socks.

So I knew the whole "running for president" thing had to have an angle. There's always an angle. The trick was figuring out what it was.

The first time I met Donald Trump, way back when, I was the back-page columnist at *Sports Illustrated*. I was playing in the AT&T Pebble Beach Pro-Am when he came at me with a bible-salesman grin and a short-fingered hand to shake. His wife, Marla Maples, was smiling at me, too.

Uh-oh, I thought. *What's this?*

"You're my favorite writer!" Trump bellowed. "I love your stuff. Tell him, Marla!"

"He does!" she said. "Look!" And she pulled out of her purse a column I'd written. Okay, there was the set-up. What was the hook?

"So," he said, "when are you going to write about ME?"

Ahh, there it was.

No problem. Trump was the most accessible, bombastic, and quotable businessman in the world. Why would I turn that down? So when I set out to write my golf book *Who's Your Caddy?*—in which I would caddy for 12 golf legends, celebrities, and oddballs—I asked if he wanted to be a chapter. "Absolutely!" he said.

When the day came, he didn't have anybody to play with, so he announced that I wouldn't be caddying for him, I'd be playing with him. Okay, you take what you can get. We played his Trump National Golf Club Westchester in Briarcliff Manor, New York, and it was like spending the day in a hyperbole hurricane.

Trump didn't just lie nonstop about himself that day. He lied nonstop about ME. He'd go up to some member and say, "This is Rick. He's the president of *Sports Illustrated*." The guy would reach out to shake my hesitant hand, but by then Trump had dragged me forward to the next member. Or secretary. Or chef. "This is Rick. He publishes *Sports Illustrated*." Before I could object, he'd go, "And this is Chef. He was voted Best Hamburger Chef in the world!" And the poor chef would look at me and shake his head with a helpless "no," same as me.

When we were alone, I finally said, "Donald, why are you lying about me?"

"Sounds better," he said.

Sounding better is Trump's m.o. It colors everything he says and does. The truth doesn't break an egg with Trump. It's all about how it sounds, how it looks, and the fact checkers can go run a 100-yard dash in a 50-yard gym.

A friend of mine had dinner with Trump and his wife, Melania, in 2015, when this whole presidential thing was starting to simmer. The husbands and wives had veered off into separate conversations. The wife said, "You have a lovely accent, Melania. Where are you from?"

"Slovenia," she said.

Trump, in mid-sentence, turned to her and interjected: "Say Austria. Sounds better."

But when I read The Big Lie, it nearly made me spit out my Cheerios. It was a tweet he'd originally posted in 2013, but I hadn't read it until his campaign began. Trump was embroiled in one of his hundreds of celebrity feuds, this one with somebody in his weight class—Dallas Mavericks owner and billionaire sports fan Mark Cuban. Cuban had dissed him on some forgettable TV show years before. "I think I said, 'I can write a bigger check than Trump right now and not even know it was missing,'" Cuban remembers.

Trump seethed about it. Trump can dish out the insults by the steam shovel but he can't take a teaspoonful back. His rule is: "When I'm attacked, I fight back 10 times harder." He vowed lifetime revenge on Cuban that day.

That's when he challenged Cuban.

Golf match? I've won 18 Club Championships including this weekend. @mcuban swings like a little girl with no power or talent. Mark's a loser

—Donald J. Trump, Twitter, March 19, 2013

Eighteen championships? That's like an NFL quarterback telling you he's won 18 Super Bowls. It's preposterous. It's a Macy's Thanksgiving Day float of a lie. Besides, Trump had already given away his little secret of how he does it that day at Westchester. "Whenever I open a new golf course," he told me, "I play the official opening round and then I just call *that* the first club

championship. There you go! I'm the first club champion!...
That's off the record, of course."

You gotta admit: It's sleazy, it's morally bankrupt, but it's
pretty clever.

I did keep it off the record, for years. But then he *kept* blud-
geoning people over the head with it.

"You know, I've won 18 club championships," he said half a
dozen times during campaign stops. "I'm a winner." As though
the trunk of his Rolls-Royce is so full of golf trophies that he can't
even get it shut.

In an interview with the *Washington Post*, he said, humbly,
"My life has been about victories. I've won a lot. I win a lot. I
win—when I do something, I win. And even in sports, I always
won. I was always a good athlete. And I always won. In golf, I've
won many club championships. Many, many club championships. And I have people that can play golf great, but they can't
win under pressure. So, I've always won."

After a big primary win, he bragged at the podium, "I know
how to win. I've won...these people will tell you. Have I won
many club championships? Does Trump know how to close?"

At another campaign stump: "Winning is winning. It's not
easy to win club championships, believe me. And I'm not talking
about with strokes. I'm talking with no strokes."

Winning 18 club championships is a lie that's so over-the-top
Crazytown it loses all credibility among golfers the second it's
out of his mouth. To double-check, I called the only guy who
could come close: George "Buddy" Marucci, of Philadelphia. Like
Trump, Marucci belongs to more clubs than you can fit in your

bag. Like Trump, he's in the right age bracket, at six years younger than Trump. Like Trump, he's got all the money he needs to play as many club championships as he can fly to. Unlike Trump, he's as fine a golfing businessman as you can find. Marucci took 19-year-old Tiger Woods—24 years his junior—to the last hole of the 1995 U.S. Amateur final before finally losing.

So, Buddy Marucci, do YOU have 18 club championships?

"Ha!" he laughed. "No way. I have a few, but nowhere near that many. It's hard to win a club championship. I might have eight. Tops."

This is a guy who's been breaking par for the past 45 years. He belongs to nearly every creamy course in the world—Winged Foot, Seminole, Pine Valley, Cypress Point. If it's on a top 10 in the world list, Marucci probably has a locker there.

"Eighteen?" he said. "I don't see how anybody could do that." When I explained to him how Trump did it, he said, "You know, I'm not sure even doing THAT I could get to 18."

When Trump told Gary Player he'd won 18 championships, Player scoffed. "I told him that if anyone beats him, he kicks them out. So, he had to win."

Was Trump's name on the wall of any clubs he *didn't* own? Nope. Was it on the walls at Trump Washington, D.C., in Virginia, a course that was already up and running when he bought it? Nope. Or Trump Jupiter, which was a Ritz Carlton course when he bought it? Nope. Was it on the wall at any of his own courses he'd opened? Oh, yes.

Trump International in West Palm Beach, Florida, has a plaque on the wall that lists all the men who've won the men's club championship. Trump appears three times: 1999, 2001, and 2009. But hold on. The course wasn't even *open* in 1999. Turns out, then White House spokesperson Hope Hicks admitted to the *Washington Post*, Trump played in a "soft opening" round on November 1 of that year with "a group of the early members" and declared it the club championship.

Congratulations?

On March 17, 2013, Trump tweeted he'd won the club championship again at Trump International. This is the one he was gloating to Cuban about.

Just won The Club Championship at Trump International Golf Club in Palm Beach-lots of very good golfers-never easy to win a C.C.

But the plaque for that year lists the winner as "Tom Roush." The catch? It wasn't really the club championship at all. Trump won the "Super Seniors Club Championship," which at most clubs is reserved for players 60 and older. Something to be proud of, sure, but not within a Super Walmart of beating the best young players in the club. The difference between "Club Champion" and "Super Senior Club Champion" is the difference between Vanna White and Betty White.

"I remember Melania used to ask us, 'What is this 'Super Seniors'?'" recalls former Trump Westchester exec Ian Gillule. "And Mr. Trump would say, 'Oh, Super Seniors is *better* than just a regular club championship, honey.' He was saying it tongue in cheek but she didn't know the difference."

I called golf writer Michael Bamberger of Golf.com. He once did a story for *Sports Illustrated* on playing every Trump course *with* Trump. Had he heard about these 18 club championships? He had.

Bamberger: "We were at Trump Westchester and Trump says, 'Michael, I just won the club championship here.' And I'm thinking, 'Wow, that's a little hard to believe, since he's about a 9 or 10 [handicap] and you don't get any strokes in the club championship.' So I said, 'Who'd you beat?' And he said, 'This guy!'" Trump was pointing to his longtime cement contractor, Lou Rinaldi, who's a zero handicap and a terrific player. Bamberger looked at Rinaldi, who shrugged his shoulders as if to say, "I'm gonna argue with my boss?"

Later, Bamberger found out that, too, was the senior club championship. "Then I found out even later," Bamberger says, "that it wasn't that year at all. It was a different year."

At Trump Bedminster in New Jersey, Trump once won a senior club championship from 87 miles away. He'd declared that the club should start having senior club championships for those 50 and up, but he forgot that one of the best players at the club had just turned 50. Having zero chance at beating the guy, he went up to his Trump Philadelphia course on the day of the tournament and played with a friend there. Afterward, according to a source inside the Bedminster club, he called the Bedminster pro shop and announced he'd shot 73 and should be declared the winner. The pro, wanting to stay employed, agreed. His name went up on the plaque. "But then," says the source, "somebody talked to the caddy up in Philly and asked him what Trump shot that day. The caddy goes, 'Maybe 82. And that might be generous.' He pulls that kind of sh*t all the time around here."

More than one source described another time when Trump happened to walk into the Bedminster clubhouse just as a worker was putting up the name of the newly crowned senior club championship winner on a wooden plaque. Trump had been out of town and hadn't played in the tournament, but when he saw the player's name, he stopped the employee. "Hey, I beat that guy all the time. Put my name up there instead." The worker was flummoxed.

"Really, sir?"

"Yeah, yeah. I beat that guy constantly. I would've beaten him. Put my name up."

Of the 18 club championship "wins" that Trump listed for *Golf Digest*, 12 are actually senior or super senior club championships. To repeat: senior and super senior club championships are not men's club championships. They're like bowling with bumpers. Besides, as I say, most of those smell like three-day-old halibut. So that leaves six *real* club championships. One of the six he lists was Trump Westchester 2001, when the club wasn't officially open yet. That leaves five. The next was Westchester 2002, when the club was only nine holes. If it really happened, you can't count that. That leaves four, one of them being Westchester in 2004. Could he have actually won that?

"Well, no, I know for a fact that's not true," Gillule says. "He never won any in the eight years I worked there. I mean, I loved working for Mr. Trump, but you know, some people take a certain license with the truth."

We do know that Trump played in the 2007 Westchester Men's Club Championship and was knocked out in the first round by a 15-year-old named Adam Levin. Trump was four-up with five holes to play, helped greatly by the 60-year-old calling two ticky-tack rule violations on the kid, one for accidentally touching the grass inside a hazard and one for fixing a small ball mark off the green, both loss-of-hole penalties.

That's when, according to Levin, Trump said to the small gallery, "The kid put up a good fight, didn't he?" A small bonfire lit under Levin, who wound up winning hole after hole, tying Trump up through 18 and then winning on the second playoff hole.

"He didn't even say 'Congratulations' or 'Good match,'" remembers Levin, now a data analyst. "He didn't look me in the eye. He just shook my hand and walked off. He'd kind of been a dick the whole day. We were together for five or six hours, so there was plenty of time for conversation with me or my parents, but all he ever said was, 'Isn't this course fantastic?' and 'Aren't these facilities the best?' He's a total asshole with no character."

That leaves three possible club championship wins, all at one course—Trump International in West Palm Beach. But we already know the 1999 win there is a lie, since the course wasn't open. That leaves two. Of those two—2001 and 2009—I have never seen a signed scorecard or spoken to any objective person who remembers him winning or not winning.

Final score on the "18 club championships": Lies 16, Incompletes 2, Confirms 0. By this time, Trump's nose has grown so long he could putt with it.

The whole thing bugged me so much I started to itch. I wasn't offended as a voter. I was offended as a *golfer*. You can't *get away* with that. You want to make political promises you can't keep? Great, knock yourself out. You want to invent tales of your cut-throat savvy in business deals? Live it up. But golf *means* something to me. I've played it my whole life. It's kept me sane and happy and found me more friends than I can count.

One of the things I love the most about golf is that you're your own referee. You call fouls on yourself. Integrity is built into the fabric of the game. Honesty is more precious in golf than the little white dimples. As Ben Crenshaw likes to say, "Golf is a game with a conscience."

For golfers, the stain of cheating is so much graver than winning or losing that we live in mortal fear of being called a cheater. Tom Watson accused Gary Player of illegally moving a leaf away from his ball at the Skins Game in 1983 and they've hardly spoken since. *One leaf.* Vijay Singh could win 10 majors and never lose his label as a cheater, based on a tiny incident that may or may not have happened once years ago in Indonesia.

So here was Trump caterwauling about 18 golf championships that were faker than Cheez Whiz, and it started to make me think. How much of what Trump says about his golf brilliance does the country believe? During the campaign, when Trump stood up in front of 30,000 red hats and bloviated, "When it comes to golf, very few people can beat me," did people buy that? Because 50 guys at every course in America can beat him.

When Trump turned his back on Puerto Rico after Hurricane Maria, did anybody know that he'd abandoned his "fabulous" golf project there the year before, a bankruptcy that left the tiny territory with a $32 million debt?

When Trump held endless 18-hole meetings at his Florida courses with this prime minister and that emperor, were these leaders returning home to laugh at OUR president the way they laughed at him at the United Nations? Would they think all Americans cheat at golf?

It got me thinking...

Somebody should point out that the way Trump does golf is sort of the way he does a presidency, which is to operate as though the rules are for other people.

Somebody should explain that facts and truth are to Trump what golf scores and crowd sizes are—"feelings"—malleable and negotiable, flitting this way and that like an arm-waving inflatable car-lot balloon man.

Somebody should write that the way Trump cheats at golf, lies about his courses, and stiffs his golf contractors isn't that far from how he cheats on his wives, lies about his misdeeds, and stiffs the world on agreements America has already made on everything from Iran to climate change.

"Golf is like bicycle shorts," I once wrote. "It reveals a lot about a man."

You could write a book about what Trump's golf reveals about him.

Here it is.

2

YOU AIN'T NO BALLERINA

Golf is fatal.
—THEODORE ROOSEVELT

FOR PRESIDENTS, THE WHITE House is a kind of prison with butlers. You can't go anywhere without a squadron of Secret Service people and a week of planning. You sleep above your office, where a desk full of the world's biggest problems silently screams for you. That's why golf is perfect for presidents. With no skyscraper windows, no streets for people to line up on, no intersections, no passing cars, presidents can stay relatively safe.

Where they play, how they play, how often and why they play can sometimes tell you more about a president than a room full of historians.

Golf didn't become trendy in America until the turn of the 20th century, and one of the first to get bit was William Howard Taft, a man who topped 300 pounds. He loved the game so much that he once blew off the president of Chile, who was waiting for him back in the White House, to keep his tee time.

Woodrow Wilson was such a worrier that his doctor *ordered* him to play golf to relieve his indigestion, even though Wilson couldn't play dead in a cowboy movie. He rarely broke 110. He'd putt hunched over 90 degrees, like a man talking to a pet mouse, with a putter that couldn't have been much taller than a toilet plunger. Wilson played only with his wife and his doctor, fearing that anybody else would want to talk about the League of Nations or somesuch. He became hopelessly addicted to the game. He even painted his golf balls black so he could play in the snow. Wilson makes Trump look like a newbie. Presidential golf historian Don Van Natta estimates Wilson might have played as many as 1,600 times during his eight years, about every other day, always first thing in the morning. He played faster than the morning train and was usually back at his desk by 9 am.

The swashbuckling Warren Harding was just the opposite. Golf to him was a kind of party with spikes. Why hurry? He loved all celebrities, but especially golf stars. He hosted the legendary night owl Walter Hagen often. One day, Hagen presented Harding with one of his favorite drivers.

"What can I do for you in return?" Harding asked, tickled.

The habitually late Hagen said it sure would be convenient to have a Secret Service badge to get him out of speeding tickets. He got it.

Harding was the first in a long line of presidents who fudged the rules. He was great fun on the golf course, long on laughs, always in plus fours and a bow tie. He wasn't above having a few belts between green and tee, which, coupled with his big off-balance lash, kept him from scoring well. Still, he was devoted to it. He was in San Francisco, on a vacation that included boat loads of golf, when he suddenly shuddered and died, probably of congestive heart failure. To commemorate him, San Francisco is now home to a terrific public golf course, Harding Park.

Calvin Coolidge wasn't good or fun or loose with golf at all and, in fact, was a chop's chop, which is to say he was so bad he couldn't even shoot his weight. When he left the White House for good, he left his clubs there.

Our most talented golfing president, by far, was Franklin Delano Roosevelt. A big hitter with a fine iron game and a diamond cutter's touch around the greens, he won many golf medals as a teen and, at 18, won the men's club championship (no, *really*) at Canada's Campobello Golf Club. But polio hit him at age 39, 12 years before he became president, and he never played again. Still, his work projects gave us dozens of terrific public tracks, including Bethpage in New York, site of the 2019 PGA Championship.

Harry Truman played piano, not golf, but his successor, Dwight Eisenhower loved it like dogs love bones. He could hardly stand to be away from his clubs. In fact, he'd stroll the halls of the White House with an iron, taking half-swings while he pondered what to do about the postwar world. He and his idol—a permanently tan heartthrob named Arnold Palmer—fueled the 1960s golf boom in this country that didn't slow down until the Great Recession of 2007.

Ike loved golf but it didn't love him. His Achilles' heel was putting. He'd approach the ball as if it were a snake, freeze like a statue over it, then jab at it and jump back fast. He seemed to have 11 kinds of yips. To practice, he built a putting green outside the Oval Office. Sometimes, upon re-entering the office, he'd forget to take off his spikes. I once crouched down there and felt the holes he left in the wooden floor.

Were it not for his bad back, President Kennedy could've been terrific. He played on the Harvard freshman golf team but hurt his back playing football and didn't go out the next year. His swing was elegant and upright, with a perfectly balanced finish, his slim right shoulder facing perfectly toward the target, his hatless hair tossed back with the wind, a kind of Gatsby in cashmere. Unlike Trump, JFK didn't want to talk about his golf, didn't want cameras around while he played it, and didn't want to announce what he shot. After his election but before his inauguration, Kennedy rattled his tee shot in and out of the cup on the 16th at Cypress Point, the most famous par 3 in the world. Kennedy breathed a sigh of relief. "You're yelling for the damn ball to go in," he said to his playing partners, "and I'm seeing a promising political career coming to an end!"

LBJ played miserably and mostly as a way to cajole congressmen to vote for this bill or that. They say he wrangled the votes he needed for his landmark Civil Rights Act on the golf course. He was fond of swear words and mulligans, taking sometimes five, six, and seven of each in a single nine holes, always reminding his opponents, "It's not nice to beat the president." After he was out of the office, he found out how true that was.

Nixon played, but never looked natural at it, always smiling too big, wearing his pants too high. His friends said he did it just to suck up to Ike as his vice president. Nixon was about an 18 handicap, but after resigning over Watergate, golf became a refuge and he got down to 12. So, you know, Watergate wasn't *all* bad.

Nixon's resignation, coupled with the resignation of his veep Spiro Agnew, shoehorned into the Oval Office the only bona-fide college sports star we've ever had, former Michigan lineman Gerald Ford. A natural athlete, President Ford loved golf, but it didn't love him. Still, he'd play as much as he could. He'd even play in the PGA Tour's Pebble Beach Pro-Am, a nightmare for the Secret Service, not to mention the galleries. Ford hit far more people with golf balls than ever voted for him for president (that number is zero), mostly because his driver was long and wrong. But he did make a hole in one once, at Colonial Country Club in Fort Worth, playing with Crenshaw in the Pro-Am. "The place went crazy," Crenshaw remembers. "He was beside himself. He turned to me said, 'I can't believe I just did that!'"

Golf went dark for a while after Ford. Jimmy Carter fished. Reagan could take golf or leave it, preferring horses. He was about a 13. You can still see his locker at Los Angeles Country Club.

There can't be a more golfy family than the Bushes. Bush 41's grandfather, George Herbert Walker Bush, was the president of the U.S. Golf Association (USGA) and invented the Walker Cup, the amateur version of the Ryder Cup. Bush 41's father, Prescott Bush, was scratch (a 0 handicap) and also president of the USGA for a year. Bush 41 was the fastest golfer I've ever seen. He was an 18 handicap with elbows flying every which way. He looked like a man trying to swat a horsefly. What he cared about more than score was finishing in less than two hours. The best-selling author James Patterson played with him once. "It was a blur," Patterson says. "The whole thing seemed to be a rush to get to the end. It was a feeling like, 'Wow, are we done now?' But he was very nice, very kind, and very down to earth."

Bush 41 loved the Texas pros like Crenshaw and Tom Kite as if they were his sons. In fact, any writer who dared criticize either of them would hear it from him personally, including yours truly. After Kite got out-captained by Seve Ballesteros in Spain at the 1997 Ryder Cup, despite having 8 of the top 14 players in the world (Europe had one), I poked a little fun at Kite. He was squiring Bush and Michael Jordan around in his plodding four-man cart while Seve was zipping hither and yon in some sort of turbo cart by Maserati, seemingly showing up at every hole, shouting instructions in Spanish, telling players which greens had been mowed *during* the round, and generally driving circles around Kite. Europe beat the United States, 14.5 to 13.5. The next week, Bush sent *Sports Illustrated* a hand-typed letter:

> Was Rick Reilly even there? Didn't he sense the comeback in the air on Sunday?...Tom Kite and the American players don't deserve the cynical, subtle put down Reilly lays on them.
>
> An America fan,
a Tom Kite fan,
G.B.

Yes, I was there. In fact, I perched next to Bush half a dozen times that day. Apparently, I didn't make much of an impression.

Bob Hope once said, "I've always enjoyed playing golf with a president. The only problem is that there are so many Secret Service men around there's not much chance to cheat." Hope would've loved playing with Bill Clinton.

When I played with Clinton in 1995 at Congressional Country Club for a story, he cheated with the *help* of the Secret Service. He didn't take mulligans, though, which are complete do-overs of a shot. No, he took what the press called "Billigans." He'd hit his first ball and tell everybody he was going to play that one. But then he'd take three, four, even five practice shots from the same place—Billigans. (Wholly illegal.) Of course, with so many balls on the hole, it started to look like an Easter egg hunt. It was hard to figure out which was his first ball. Luckily, the Secret Service seemed to always know: the one near the pin. What agent doesn't want to be ambassador to Sweden?

Clinton didn't seem to give a fig about the four SWAT guys in the trees or the six agents walking with us, all of them Uzi'd up under their sport coats. We also had 13 golf carts following us, one of which held the red phone, one the assistant to the chief of staff, and one the chief of protocol. I don't know how the chief of protocol would've liked what Clinton said to me as we walked past a balcony full of people waving to us. He was waving with his right hand and elbowing me in the ribs with the left.

"What?" I said out of the side of the mouth.

"You see the blond on the left?"

"Yeah?"

"I just got a wink from her."

I wanted to say, "They *did* mention I was a reporter, right?"

Like Trump, Clinton was fabulous golf company. Unlike Trump, he wanted the round to last as long as humanly possible. A six-hour round was delirium for Clinton: more cigars, more laughing, less Bosnia. He zinged you, slapped you on the back, and praised you, sometimes all in one par 3. He was oddly conversant on anything golf. "You like that new bubble shaft?" he asked me. (I didn't even realize I *had* one.) He had a complicated swing you'd never be able to find parts for—moving here and there, up and down, left and right. At impact, he'd jump up on the balls of his feet, like Andre Agassi hitting a forehand, and it produced a big cutting slice. This, plus the 24 clubs he had in his bag (the limit is 14), plus all the chasing down of the errant Billigans, was more than the caddy, a 70-year-old black gentlemen, could handle.

"Get off your toes!" he finally said. "You ain't no damn ballerina!"

The chief of protocol's mouth fell open like a drawbridge. The necks of the Secret Service agents snapped. There was an awkward pause. Then Clinton just said, "You're right. My bad." With all the Billigans and craziness, it was hard to tell what he shot, but the card said 82, which he told me later was the best of his life.

(Quick story about Trump and the Clintons: One time, Hillary gets her brother, Hugh Rodham, on at Winged Foot, even though neither are members. Rodham shows up wearing shorts. That's a no-no at Winged Foot. Pants only. Hugh Rodham is a man of large girth, so there weren't any pants in the pro shop that fit. The valet says to a caddy, "Go in and get Mr. Rodham a pair of rain pants to wear." The caddy goes in, tries to think of a guy near to Rodham's size, goes to Trump's locker, gets his rain pants, and runs out. Rodham plays in the rain pants. When this story gets back to Trump, he flips out. He makes Winged Foot buy him an entirely new rain suit. *Clinton cooties*.)

The greatest day for presidential golf buffs was February 15, 1995, the only time three presidents have played in one group. It was at the Bob Hope Desert Classic—standing president Clinton, Bush 41, and Ford, with Hope thrown in as a foursome filler. It was a unique moment. I always fantasize that at one point Hope said, "You're on the tee, Mr. President," and three guys knocked heads trying to tee up their ball.

Bush shot 93, Clinton 95, and Ford 103. And we know those scores are real. It was on NBC. Bush, though, was a menace to the gallery. On the first hole, he ricocheted one off a tree and hit an elderly woman on her nose, breaking her glasses and splattering blood everywhere. On the 14th, he hit a man on the back of the leg. His wife Barbara shook her head and said, "As if we don't have enough violence on television."

Bush 43 was a fair golfer—about a 15—but he stopped playing golf in 2003 out of "solidarity" with soldiers in the war. No, he actually did. What would it take to get Trump to stop playing? Nuclear winter?

"The Bushes don't cheat," Crenshaw avers. "Forty-three will get to the first tee and say, 'Now look, I'm not moving this ball today. I'm playing it honestly all the way through.' And he would."

Crenshaw became so close with Bush 43 that one year, when he was playing the PGA Tour's Kemper Open near Washington,

43 insisted he stay at the White House. After the first round, though, Crenshaw, famously awful at directions, got lost coming back to the White House and ended up parked on the side of the highway, wrestling a map. A patrolman pulled up and asked where he was trying to go.

"Well, uh, you're not gonna believe this," Crenshaw stammered, red-faced. "But I'm stayin' at the White House."

When the cop stopped laughing, he escorted him there personally.

Obama loved golf and liked to play it with—are you ready for this?—sportswriters. I kid you not. He played dozens of times with ESPN *Pardon the Interruption* hosts Michael Wilbon and Tony Kornheiser. Obama is a feverish sports nut, so it was a good fit. I know, because he was my fantasy football partner for an ESPN column once. He knew more than I imagined.

"We need a wide receiver," I'd say. "Let's pick (so and so)."

"No way," he'd say. "They just lost their receivers coach."

You could've put Obama's golf on a USGA poster—no cheating, no mulligans, no do-overs. He also kept it very private. He rarely played with politicians or world leaders, mostly guys from his travel advance team, especially as he was trying to get better. After a year and a half out of office, he was down to an 11 handicap, according to Wilbon. "I'm not a hack, but I'm not quitting my day job," he likes to say now. Off the tee he's "very straight," Tiger Woods says, but "not long." His chipping is salty, but he's a disaster in the bunkers. Like Saddam Hussein, he may someday get in a bunker and never get out.

Which brings us to Trump.

No president has been as up to his clavicles in golf as Donald Trump. None has been woven so deeply into the world of golf. Trump doesn't just play courses; he builds them, buys them, owns them, operates them, sues over them, lies about them, bullies with them, and brags about them. From the people he knows, to the businesses he runs, to the favors he hands out, to the access he grants, to the trouble he gets into, to the places he goes, to the money he makes, to the money he loses, to the opinions it informs in his brain, Trump's soul is practically dimpled.

But keep on your toes, ballerinas, because it's a wild dance.

3

THE KID WITH THE BIG SHEKELS

You gotta watch those guys at Cobbs Creek. They'll take your teeth.
—DONALD J. TRUMP

IF YOU WERE BORN a son of Fred Trump, you heard one thing over and over: *Win, win, and then win some more. Whatever you have to do, be a winner.* Fred Trump constantly urged his boys to be "killers." Life as a Trump was not about hugs or picnics or bedtime reading. It was about winning. Nothing else mattered.

"The stories you hear about Fred," says Jack O'Donnell, vice president of Trump Plaza Casino from 1987 to 1990, "he was pretty rough on the boys—win, win, win, strict, strict, strict—always finish on top. That's not easy."

Donald took to sports and no wonder. Every day, sports gave young Donald the chance to prove to his father he was a winner. A naturally good athlete—"I was always the best athlete," he once boasted, "Nobody ever talks about that"—Trump likes to say that at one time he could've been a pro baseball player. "But those weren't good times for baseball in terms of, you make $2," he told golf podcaster David Feherty. So he chose a career in real estate instead. So, to recap: Major League Baseball was dying to get Donald Trump, but they weren't paying enough to suit him, so he broke their heart and joined his dad's business.

It's no wonder Trump fell in love with golf. Every round of golf comes with 18 chances to win, plus the 19th chance—my final score versus yours. *I beat you. I win. You're a loser.* Trump's love affair with golf has far outlasted any romance he's had with any woman or career or party affiliation.

Fred, a second-generation German, played, but only rarely. One day when Trump was young, his dad took him out to a golf course called Forest Park near Queens. Young Donald didn't play that day but says his father "was, potentially, a very good golfer. He probably only played 10 times in his life, but he had a beautiful swing."

Donald himself didn't take up the game with passion until college in the late 1960s, and I could give you 1,000 guesses where and you'd never get it.

It was Philadelphia's scruffy Cobbs Creek, aka "The Crick," a goulash of gamblers and hustlers and out-of-work steelworkers. It was a public track, full of $2 weekend hacks and $100/hole sharpies and Penn students. One of those students was Trump, who'd drive the 10 minutes from Penn's Wharton School of Business to play it with his buddies. "I remember Trump," says Bob Steele, 76, a Cobbs "Cricker" since 1962. "He didn't sneak on. He paid. You could tell the kid came from big shekels. I remember he was always yakkin'. Good-lookin' guy, though. He stood out from the rest of 'em. Well dressed, you know? When he ran for president, I saw him on TV and I said, 'Hey! That guy was a Cricker!' "

If you were a true Cricker, you bet on everything before, during, and after the round, and then bought a cold beer from out of the trunk of Cornbread's car, sat under the trees, and laughed and argued about it until dark. They played for knee-knocking amounts for the time—$50 Nassaus. Carry-over skins. Pig and Wolf. Vegas. If you could think of a bet, somebody would give you action. And not just golf bets. One time, a guy named Lou bet he could carry two guys and their bags on his back up the 100-yard hill at 17—and did.

So it was that the millionaire's son learned the game among the carpenters and bus drivers and spike-shoed grifters on a course that needed a shave and a clean shirt. "I had friends that were golfers," Trump told *Golf Digest*. "I'd never played golf—I always played baseball and football and stuff. And so I'd go out to Cobbs Creak…a public course, a rough course, no grass on the tees, no nothing, but it was good, and great people. All hustlers out there. I mean, more hustlers than any place I've seen to this day. I played golf with my friends, and then I started to play with the hustlers. And I learned a lot. I learned about golf, I learned about gambling. I learned about everything."

They were expensive lessons. Says Steele: "The hustlers here, man, they'd see some yokel show up in a panama hat asking for a game and they'd send the poor guy home without even hamburger money."

There were Row Boat and Frankie and a dozen other guys, unafraid to break the rules to break your wallet. Even pioneering black pro and consummate hustler Charlie Sifford would show up now and then. This was a place full of guys with holes in their pockets, the better to drop an extra ball when nobody was looking. And when they were out of sheep to fleece, they'd fleece each other.

"One time, Frankie was playing another hustler for $50," remembers Steele. "So it's tied up on 18. The guy Frankie is playing hooks it left into the long gunch and can't find it. All of a sudden, the hustler goes, 'Hey! I found it!' Frankie comes running over, pissed. 'You slob! How you gonna find your ball when it's in my pocket?!?'"

As a Cricker, Trump learned (a) it's not cheating if you don't get caught; (b) if you trash talk enough, your opponent might choke; and (c) the best stroke in golf is the one where your opponent writes you a check.

At the Crick, he honed a swing with a powerful move through the ball. It starts way, way inside and so flat it's almost parallel to the ground. But on the downswing, he gets it back on plane, then slams violently through the ball, propelled by a furious turn of the hips, the kind of hip turn you rarely see in amateurs, nearly Sam Snead-like, with a big follow through. He's a president who gets off bombs. "He outdrove me every time," Bill Clinton once lamented.

"For me, it's all about the hips," he once told *Golf Digest's* Jaime Diaz. "Just get them out of the way as fast and as hard as I can and let the arms really swing through. I read about the hips a long time ago in Ben Hogan's book, and it became my simple key, and I've stayed with it. It might look a little crazy, but the more I clear, the straighter I hit it."

"What most impressed me," Tiger Woods blogged after playing him, "was how far he hits the ball at 70 years old. He takes a pretty good lash."

Unfortunately, the rest of his game isn't nearly as good. Former tour star and now Fox golf analyst Brad Faxon played with Trump in West Palm Beach. "He's good off the tee, hits this nice draw every time," Faxon says. "His irons are OK. He's a poor chipper. He'll do anything not to chip, so he'll putt anytime he can, even out of bunkers if he can, around water. He's an OK putter. He's a 4 [handicap] tee to green and a 20 [handicap] chipper."

"I'm pretty much a natural golfer," Trump has said, humbly.

Golf + Trump is an odd couple, because in golf the most revered thing is not winning but honor. Jack Nicklaus may be the game's greatest winner, but The King will always be Arnold Palmer, for the way he showed kindness to princes and plumbers alike. Bobby Jones was so taken with the idea of honor that he refused to turn pro, despite winning seven majors. Wasn't gentlemanly. It wasn't until Tiger Woods that the idea of scorched-earth winning came along. Woods' father, Earl, once told me they used to have a mantra they repeated after every victory: "We came. We saw. We won. We got the fuck out of town."

Still, Woods would rather finish last than cheat. Every day, in every tournament, in every state, players report violations on themselves that nobody else saw. Hale Irwin once missed the playoff at the 1983 British Open by one shot because he says he whiffed a one-inch putt on the final day. Nobody saw it but Irwin. In golf, that's enough. Not long ago, a South Dakota high schooler named Kate Wynja was about to win the state championship in a rout when she realized she'd signed for a 4 on a hole when she'd actually made a 5. Nobody else knew. Wouldn't have made a lick of difference in the outcome. But she immediately told officials, who had no choice but to disqualify her. She lost not only the individual title but her team's state title. Even Jack Nicklaus himself was impressed. He tweeted:

Congrats to this young lady for using golf as a vehicle to teach us all life lessons on honesty and integrity.

In golf, you don't cheat your opponent. You don't cheat your friends. You don't cheat, period. But somehow—either from his father drilling into his brain or the Crickers drilling into his wallet—this was lost on Trump. "Win or else" flattened "honor of the game" in a one-round knockout. Trump had to win, no matter what, and those great spaces of golf allowed him the cover to do it.

"He found a game that suits him to a T," says O'Donnell. "He has such a short attention span that makes golf perfect for him. You stand on the tee box for a minute and chat, then you hit, then you go your own way. It's very short periods of concentration.

But the best part is that it's all self-regulated. He can cheat any time he wants."

When college was over, he took all that to the country clubs, where Trump figured out that not only could he pencil-whip his very un-Crick opponents even easier, but his quick charm and solid game could also help him grease the rails to the top.

"There was this [New York] banker who was really going to do bad numbers on me," Trump told Golf Channel's David Feherty on a podcast, referring to his Atlantic City casino bankruptcies. "I was playing one day and we needed another person. Here's this [banker] at the course. They said to him, 'Would you like to join the group?'...He was a terrible golfer, terrible....Now, I'm in deep trouble. I owe this man tens of tens of millions of dollars. So he topped his first ball, topped his second ball. This goes on for two or three more holes. I finally said, 'Do me a favor. Take your hands in a V, point the V to the shoulder. Strengthen your grip.' He had a terrible weak grip. The guy winds up hitting the nicest ball of his life. It goes out to the right and hooks back into the fairway. He says, 'I've never hit a shot like that! That's the nicest shot I've ever hit!' He ends up playing the best he's ever played.... So he sees me the next day and says, 'Hey, can we work this out over lunch?' And I worked it out with him in about 10 minutes. So, who knows, without golf, maybe I wouldn't be sitting here!"

No other sport captivated Trump like golf. He became addicted to the constant competition, hole by hole, day by day. And not just the bets. He came to see his handicap as a kind of contest, too, one he has to win daily.

"I'd say he's a solid 7," says Trump's permanent caddy at his Washington course, A.J. (He prefers I don't give his last name.) "He really gets through it. He can drive it a long way. For a 72-year-old man, he's amazing. He has a little trouble around the greens, but he can flop it [hit a very high and soft chip] from anywhere. He's amazing with the flop. He can have his hot putting days, too. Sometimes, not so much."

"I'd say he's a legit 10," Faxon says. "He'll probably get mad at me for that, but I think that's about right." Four-time major winner Ernie Els played with him and declared him to be "an 8 or a 9." LPGA great Annika Sörenstam has played with him at least twice and says, "I would say he's a 9 or 10."

So the caddy and the pros who make a living in the game estimate his handicap to be somewhere between a 7 and a 10. The only problem with all that is Trump *insists* his handicap is a 2.8. In the world of golf handicaps, that difference is huge. If Trump is a 2.8, Queen Elizabeth is a pole vaulter. No possible way. It would take a 9 handicap five good years of hard practice to get to a 2.8 and Donald Trump doesn't practice.

Former Republican Speaker of the Florida House Will Weatherford played with Trump in 2015 at Southern Highlands Golf Club in Las Vegas, the day of the Floyd Mayweather–Manny Pacquiao fight. "He was a lot of fun," Weatherford recalls. "When you play with Donald, you do a lot of listening. He was telling stories, entertaining us the whole way around."

Was he a stickler about the rules?

"Not so much. I remember on one par 3, he hit his first shot way out of bounds. Teed up another and I think that one was lost, too. The third one landed about 12 feet from the hole. He made that putt. I'm pretty sure he gave himself a 2 on that hole. Look, I take mulligans, too. I'm not judging....But then later, he was apparently telling people he was a 2 or a 3 and that they should call Will Weatherford and I'd confirm what a great golfer he is. I mean, if he's a 2, that's news to me. I've played with 2s and that didn't look anything like a 2."

What was he then?

"Well, I'm about a 12 or 13 and I wouldn't say he was any better than me."

When you look up Trump on GHIN.com—the USGA's online handicap search site—he's listed as a 2.8. But, as of press time, he'd only posted 20 times in the past seven years. Seven years? For an avid golfer like Trump, that's preposterous. In golf, honor demands that you post every round, good or bad, high or low, so that the bets are fair. You finish your round, shake hands, go straight to the computer, post your score, pay off the bet, and then drink your beer, in that order. If people see that you don't post your scores, your phone is going to stop ringing. Even the people Trump plays with post their scores. In 2016 alone, Rudy Giuliani posted 16 times. Tony Russo, a noted Washington lobbyist, posted 20 times just in the summer of 2018. Anybody who only plays three times a year would be a 22.8, not a 2.8. We know the 2.8 is a lie because, as president, he's averaging about 80 rounds a year, according to TrumpGolfCount.com, a slavish accounting of Trump's golf activity. If he's playing an average of

80 rounds a year, and only posting 3 rounds, that means he's leaving 95% of them off.

So what's he doing? He's cherry picking. He's only putting in his showiest rounds. Even with the scores he posts, he's either shaving multiple shots off his total or inflating the difficulty of the courses he played. The GHIN system takes your 20 most recent scores, throws out the worst 10, and averages the best 10, factoring in course rating and course slope. But take a look at those 20 scores:

- He posted only one score in all of 2016, and two in 2015. So which do you believe? The Trump who says he's great at golf, who wants you to vote for him because he's a golf champion, who tweets about playing golf all the time? Or this Trump, who apparently only plays every time Germany wins a war?

- Look at the "slopes" of his scores. Slope is the relative difficulty of a course. The computer is much more impressed with the 100 you shot on a 130 slope course than the 100 you shot on a 115 course. The average course slope is about 120. Fifteen of the 20 scores Trump posted were on courses with slopes of over 140. Anything over 140 is insanely hard. That's like a skier who only goes down double black diamonds. Only the most sadistic courses in America are over 140. Just to give you an idea, Augusta National is a 137. Bethpage Black in New York is harder than Chinese algebra, and it's only 144. I play once a week on some pretty good courses, and the highest slope out of my last 20 is 135. So Trump could be tricking the GHIN computer by plugging in the slope of the way-back pro tees—even though everyone says he plays the normal tees—to make whatever score he shot look more impressive to the computer, which drives his handicap lower. Again, it's dirty and unscrupulous but—you gotta admit—kind of genius.

- He posted a 68 in October of 2017, and then deleted it. Now, do you know any golfers who would delete a 68? Most would get the scorecard blown up and make wallpaper.

So why go to such lengths to gin up a fake 2.8 handicap? What's so bad about being a 9? According to the National Golf Foundation, only around 3% of men over 70 are single-digit handicaps. Most 70-somethings would give their dentures for that. Why must he pretend he's a 3, a phony number he can't

Date	Score	Course Rating/ Slope	Differential
6/16	77	72.4/134	3.9
5/15	85	73.0/144	9.4
5/15	81	71.6/140	7.6
10/14	86	74.7/149	8.6
10/14	84	74.7/149	7.1
7/14	75	69.5/137	4.5
7/14	83	71.8/135	9.4
6/14	78	72.2/137	4.8
6/14	77	73.1/143	3.1
6/14	76	71.9/139	3.3
8/13	70	72.3/147	-1.8
7/13	76	70.2/132	5.0
6/13	79	73.0/144	4.7
6/13	79	71.6/140	6.0
7/12	76	73.9/144	1.6
6/11	74	73.0/144	0.8
5/11	83	74.7/149	6.3
5/11	83	74.7/149	6.3
4/11	84	74.7/149	7.1
9/09	85	74.7/149	7.8

*Self-reported

play to from the red tees? Put it this way: Jack Nicklaus is a 3.4 on GHIN.com. If you needed a partner for a death match, loser cleans the Fallujah Denny's with a toothbrush for the rest of his life, would you take Trump or Jack Nicklaus?

So why isn't being a 9 good enough for Trump?

Because, as you're about to find out, "good enough" is never good enough for Donald Trump.

4

PELE

He cheats like hell.

—Suzann Pettersen, LPGA golfer

I USED TO HAVE this coach who told us, "How you do one thing is how you do everything. You loaf in practice, you're gonna loaf in the game. You cheat on your tests, you're gonna cheat on your wife."

I've found that to be true with golf. The guy who plays slowly on the course is going to be molasses in meetings. The guy who's generous with compliments on the course is going to do the same at dinner. And the guy who cheats on the course is going to cheat in business, or on his taxes or, say, in politics.

Jack O'Donnell worked with Trump for four years as vice president of Trump Plaza Casino in Atlantic City. O'Donnell's dad was one of the founders of Sawgrass, the iconic Pete Dye golf course near Jacksonville, Florida. "My dad always told us to respect the game," O'Donnell says. "That's the one part of the game that tells me what kind of person you are. You play the ball where it lies." So when O'Donnell's office colleague, the late Mark Eddis, came back after his first round with Trump, O'Donnell couldn't resist asking.

"So, does he improve his lie?"

Eddis looked at him and threw his head back in laughter. "Every shot but the tee shot."

Trump doesn't just cheat at golf. He cheats like a three-card Monte dealer. He throws it, boots it, and moves it. He lies about his lies. He fudges and foozles and fluffs. At Winged Foot where Trump is a member, the caddies got so used to seeing him kick his ball back onto the fairway they came up with a nickname for him: "Pele."

"I played with him once," says Bryan Marsal, longtime Winged Foot member and chair of the coming 2020 Men's U.S. Open. "It was a Saturday morning game. We go to the first tee and he couldn't have been nicer. But then he said, 'You see those two guys? They cheat. See me? I cheat. And I expect *you* to cheat because we're going to beat those two guys today.'...So, yes, it's true, he's going to cheat you. But I think Donald, in his heart of hearts, believes that *you're gonna cheat him*, too. So if it's the same, if everybody's cheating, he doesn't see it as really cheating."

Okay, but...

a) Everybody *isn't* cheating. Except for an occasional mulligan on the first tee and accepting a gimme (a short conceded putt) from an opponent, 85% of casual golfers play by the rules, according to the National Golf Foundation.

b) To say "Donald Trump cheats" is like saying "Michael Phelps swims." He cheats at the highest level. He cheats when people are watching, and he cheats when they aren't. He cheats whether you like it or not. He cheats because that's *how* he plays golf, that's how he learned it, that's how he needs it, and whether you're his pharmacist or Tiger Woods, if you're playing golf with him, he's going to cheat.

In fact, he *did* cheat with Tiger Woods. Not long after becoming president, he invited Woods, Dustin Johnson (the No. 1 player in the world at the time), and longtime Tour pro and Fox golf analyst Brad Faxon to play.

They set up a bet: Faxon and Trump against Woods and Johnson. But because Woods and Johnson are so preposterously long off the tee, they decided Faxon and Trump could tee off the middle tees. Trump would get a stroke subtracted on the eight hardest holes; everybody else would play scratch. Off they went.

"On this one hole, Donald hits his second and fats it into the water," Faxon remembers. "But he quickly says to me, 'Hey, throw me another ball; they weren't looking.' So I do. But he fats that one into the water, too. So he drives up and drops where he should've dropped the first time and hits it on the green."

Meanwhile, on the other side of the fairway, Woods, being Woods, has hit his approach to a foot from the hole for a kick-in birdie. Everybody's on the green now, with Trump about 20 feet from the hole, and getting a stroke. Trump said, "So, where does everybody stand here?"

FAXON: "Well, Tiger just made a three. What's that [putt] for, Mr. President?"

TRUMP: "Four for a three."

Faxon had to laugh because Trump was actually putting for a seven, but he was claiming it was for a four, which would've worked out to a three with his free stroke on the hole.

"How great is that?" Faxon recalled. "Four for a three! But he missed it anyway. It was really fun to play with him. He rakes [picks up] every putt [as if it's conceded], but you kind of want him to. You've heard so much about it, it's almost like you want to witness it so you can tell the stories."

One time an old country singer/songwriter friend of mine played golf with Trump in L.A. for the first time. On the very first hole, Trump kicked his ball from the rough onto the fairway. This stopped the singer cold.

"Wait a second," he yelled. "So this is how it's going to be today, Donald?"

"Oh," Trump explained. "All the guys I play with throw it out of the rough. You have to do it just to keep up with them."

Just for the record, I've played for 50 years and only know one guy who does that. His picture is on the cover.

Once, Trump hosted three famous ESPN football announcers—Mike Tirico (now with NBC), Jon Gruden (now the Raiders coach), and Ron (Jaws) Jaworski, the old Eagles quarterback—at one of his courses. Trump loves to show off his courses to celebrities, and the more celebrated you are, the more he wants you to see them and the more he wants his members to see you. Trump arrived as the other three were warming up and he picked the teams immediately. "It's gonna be me and Gruden, 'cause I like winners."

Off they went. At one point, they were playing a blind par 5, and Tirico, who's a 12.3 handicap, had 230 yards into the green.

He hit the 3-wood of his life. "Oh my god!" his caddy said, open-mouthed. The thing had the flag covered from the start. It crested the hill perfectly and was going to be tight to the pin. Shocked at his sudden skill, Tirico high-fived his caddie and strode toward the green, his shoes barely touching the grass.

But, somehow, when they got there, the ball wasn't near the pin. It wasn't even on the green. It was 50 feet *left* of the pin, in the bunker. Unless it hit a drone and ricocheted sideways, there was no physical way it could've ended up there.

"Lousy break," Trump said to Tirico, who checked the marking on the ball to be sure it was his. It was. Befuddled, it took Tirico two swipes to escape the bunker on the way to a 7.

"Afterwards," Tirico remembers, "Trump's caddy came up to me and said, 'You know that shot you hit on the par 5? It was about 10 feet from the hole. Trump threw it into the bunker. I watched him do it.'"

What did Tirico do? He laughed, shook his head, went inside, and paid Trump his money. When it comes to golf, Trump is the tornado and you are the trailer.

But why? Why does Trump cheat so much when he's already a decent player? And how can he be so shameless as to cheat right in front of people? They call him on it, but he just shrugs and cheats some more. It's ruined his reputation in the golf world. Ninety percent of the people I interviewed—on and off the record—say he openly cheats. A lot of them said they stopped playing with him because of it. So why? Why cheat? Why lie? Why exaggerate his handicap, his scores, his club championships?

"Because he has to," says Harvard psychiatrist Dr. Lance

Dodes, co-author of *The Dangerous Case of Donald Trump.* "He *needs* to be the best at everything. He can't stand not winning, not being the best. It had to have started very early in his development. To him, not being the best is like fingernails on the blackboard to you. He can't live with it.... He exaggerates his golf scores and his handicap for the same reason he exaggerates everything. He has to. He exhibits all the traits of a narcissistic personality disorder. People with his disorder have no conscience about it. He has no sense of morality about things. He lacks empathy towards others. He's a very ill man. He doesn't get that other people have rights and feelings. Other people just don't matter to him."

Trump consistently says he doesn't cheat. "I never touch the ball," he says. That's sort of true, maintains actor Anthony Anderson. "I'm not going to say Trump cheats. But if Trump's caddy cheats for him, is *that* cheating?"

"We clearly saw him hook a ball into a lake at Trump National [Bedminster]," actor Samuel L. Jackson once recalled, "and his caddy told him he found it!"

LPGA player Suzann Pettersen, a friend of Trump's, thinks he must pay his caddy extremely well "since no matter how far into the woods he hits the ball, it's in the middle of the fairway when we get there."

You can try to fight against it, but you'll fail. The first time L.A. Clippers coach Doc Rivers played with him, Trump was on the other team and his buddy was going to be Trump's partner. The buddy came over to console him. "He's like, 'Well, that's it. You've got no chance of winning today.' I figured he was trash talking. I'm like, 'Okay, let's see what you got!' But then I saw the way

Trump cheats. About the fifth or sixth hole, I went up to my buddy and said, 'I finally see what you mean. I've got no chance.'"

Boxer Oscar De La Hoya says he witnessed him cheat. Rocker Alice Cooper, too. New Jersey native Bill Rayburn wrote to me on Facebook about it. "I caddied for him once at a celebrity thing. Even with a gallery, marshals and me standing there, he openly cheated at least 10 times in the round. I finally stopped counting around the 15th hole.... He kicked his ball away from tree stumps, improved his lie, grounded his club in traps, and on the green repeatedly cheated on his ball marking, making sure to get his ball closer to the cup.... Trump walked off the 18th hole trumpeting his score, 74. Which easily was closer to 90 in the real world. Then he tipped me $10."

It's so brazen you almost admire it. When Trump and I played together that day at Westchester for *Who's Your Caddy?*, he took "floating mulligans" and re-dos, and simply subtracted shots when it came time for me to write his score down. "I have to take a newspaper 4 once in awhile," he said.

I also heard "I'm-taking-a-mulligan" excuses like:

"You distracted me."

"That bird flew over just as I was about to hit."

"My foot slipped."

The man even took a gimme chip-in that day. A "gimme" is usually a putt that your opponent concedes you will make. He says, "That's good," meaning, "I concede that you'll make that putt, so just pick it up." Gimmes are illegal under the rules of golf but as common on the course as hot dogs. Still, a gimme should not be longer than two feet, three feet tops.

Gimmes are supposed to be like gifts: they can only be given, never taken. Except for Trump. When you're playing with Trump, he has the only gimme vote. He'll declare any putt he has under five or six or eight feet a "gimme" and scoop it up. But as *you* go to pick your shorter putt up, too, he stops you and warns that "you better brush that in." He's the conductor of the Trump Train and you're just hanging on to the caboose.

The Olympic hockey star Mike Eruzione played with Trump in Palm Beach the day of Barbara Bush's funeral, an event Trump was uninvited to. Eruzione says Trump is "so much fun" to play golf with partly because you can needle him. "We're playing along," Eruzione recalls, "and I finally said, 'Mr. President, you're a very talkative guy, but I haven't once heard you say, 'That one's good, Mike.'"

But never in the history of golf has anyone taken a gimme *chip-in* until Trump did that day with me. I was in the hole for a 5 and he was lying OFF the green in 5, and he said, casually, "Well, I guess that makes this good," and he scooped the ball up.

I was gobsmacked. We were playing a $10 medal bet—i.e., a total-score bet—so every shot counted. Even if he could've chipped it close—which he wouldn't have—he'd have made a 7.

"Did you just take a gimme chip-in?" I asked, dumbfounded.

"Well, yeah, 'cause you were already in for 5."

By the time I got my jaw refastened, he was driving off in the cart. I put the scene in my book. When he was running for president, the *Washington Post* asked him about that gimme chip-in. Trump had a very odd answer: "I don't do gimme chip shots. If I asked his approval, that's not cheating, number one. Number two, I never took one."

So that clears THAT up.

In the end, the scorecard said he beat me. The rules had been pulverized into Gerber's pea puree by then, so I paid up the $10. Then he bought lunch. It's not the money; it's the winning.

"I played with him once at Trump L.A.," says Ken Slutsky, a golf executive and investor. "At the end he said, 'You owe me $27.' I said, 'Donald, you cheated on every single hole. I'm not paying you a dime.' He just kind of shrugged and left. He didn't seem to care."

Trump's cheating during a round is legendary, but his cheating after the round is just as sharp. His score always gets what I call the Trump Bump. He may wrap up a very sketchy 77 at noon. On the ride home, it'll be 75. By dinner, 72.

It's not just his score that gets the Trump Bump. It's anybody's score he likes. The legendary golfer Lee Trevino tells about the time he played one of Trump's courses, shot a 72, and then ran into Trump in the locker room.

"What'd you fire?" Trump asks.

"Seventy-two," Trevino says.

Trump is delighted and wants to start introducing the legend around his clubhouse. "This is the great Lee Trevino. He just shot a 70!" For the next person, it was, "You know who this is? Lee Trevino! He just shot a 68!" Then it was, "He just shot a 66!"

Says Trevino, "I had to get out of there before I broke the course record!"

It's not just golf scores that get the Trump Bump. It's also net worth, crowd sizes, body weight—up or down—whatever makes him the winner.

Even his buildings. His 68-story Trump Tower in New York City, for instance, isn't really 68 stories. It's 58. There's a story in the stories. When Trump Tower was finished, his 664-foot building came up 41 feet shorter than the nearby 705-foot GM Building. Trump thought, well, his first 19 floors are commercial, what was to keep him from listing the first residential floor as the 30th, instead of the 20th? If he did that, he could add 10 floors instantly, and the top floor would be listed as the 68th, which would make it at least sound taller than the 50-floor GM Building. So that's what he did. He liked the idea so much he did it for his 90-story Trump World Tower (actually 70 stories), too.

It seems a harmless kind of lie, but it caused a problem for NYC firemen in April of 2018, when a Trump Tower apartment caught fire. The information the 911 operator was getting was that the fire was on the 50th floor. But firemen on the street counted only 40 floors up to the flames. Were there two fires? What the hell was going on?

I'm 6-foot-1. I've stood next to Trump many times and we're always eye to eye. I also stand eye to eye with Barack Obama. When you look at pictures of Obama and Trump together, they're about eye to eye. It all jibes. Yet when the White House doctor announced Trump's size and weight in January of 2018, Trump was suddenly "6-3, 239 pounds." That height and weight conveniently kept Trump one-tenth of one body mass index point from being categorized as "obese." At his true 6-1 height, he'd have had to weigh 12 pounds less to avoid The Big O. Now, it's possible that Trump grew two inches since the last time I stood with him, but, since he's in his 70s, it seems unlikely.

Sometimes, the White House Trump Bumps for him. Remember short-lived White House Director of Communications Anthony Scaramucci? On his first day on the job, The Mooch was trying to illustrate how competitive Trump is. "I have seen him throw a dead spiral through a tire," Scaramucci said, according to reporters who recorded the session. "I've seen him at Madison Square Garden, with a topcoat on, standing in the key and he's hitting foul shots and swishing them. He sinks three-foot putts. I don't see this guy as a guy that's ever under siege. This is a very, very competitive person." All that was fine until the White House released the transcript of Scaramucci's briefing. Somehow, the "three-foot putts" had turned into "thirty-foot putts."

Trump often ballyhoos the 68 he says he shot once at a famous and difficult Los Angeles country club course, which would be some incredible feat, even for a vanity 3-handicap like Trump. It's a course that's tighter than Chris Christie's underwear, full of peril, tricky greens, and bunkers deep enough to hide a Mack truck. So when Trump came barreling up to the clubhouse one afternoon bragging he'd just shot a 68, it was instantly met with swimming pools of skepticism. "No way," members sitting on the porch at 18 said to him.

But there's a reason Trump's friends call him Double Down.

"Yes, I did," he said. "And it was a *legit* 68, too."

Is there any other kind?

The head pro at this particular club is a rules stickler. He serves as a rules official for the PGA of America. He would sooner play in five-inch marabou heels than commit a rules violation. As soon as Trump left, he immediately summoned the two caddies for the group into his office. The two caddies, still in their white overalls, came in and sat down. The pro closed the door.

"So," he said. "Mr. Trump says he shot 68 here today. Is that true?"

The two caddies looked at each other.

"No way," said one.

"No f*cking way," said the other.

"Seventy-nine at BEST," said the first.

The 68, they said, came with tosses, kicks, and golf balls getting free rides back to the short grass. It came with do-overs, takeovers, and floating mulligans. It came with very little sounds of plastic balls actually going into little plastic cups. "He played really well that day, but I don't think he shot a 68," says longtime NBA and college basketball coach Mike Dunleavy, who was in the group. "There was some moving of balls around, some other stuff." There was so much trickery and fraud, it was impossible to know what he'd really shot. Somewhere in the high 70s, they'd give him. For anybody else, high 70s on that course would've been a save-the-scorecard kind of day. For Trump, it wasn't nearly enough.

Longtime Los Angeles player and caddy Greg Puga, the 2000 U.S. Mid-Amateur champion, has had Trump in his group plenty. He's heard about the 68—it's a staple of L.A. caddy rooms—and he isn't buying a thimble of it. "Sixty-eight?" Puga says. "There? You gotta be kidding me. I could take him to the Long Beach Putt-Putt and he's not shooting 68. No way. No how. Not ever."

To turn a 78 into a 68, you need some clever tricks. Trump has two sleeves full.

*The Invisible Dunk

"I've played with him a lot," says a frequent guest in Trump's foursomes. "This one time, I was in the fairway and he was right of the green but a little bit down the hill. He didn't think anybody was watching, but I was. I saw him make a chipping motion from the side of the hill but no ball came up. Then he walked up the hill, stuck his hand in the hole and pulled a ball out. It must've been a ball he had in his hand the whole time. Then he looked up and yelled, 'I chipped in!' I mean, who does that?"

*The Quick Rake

This is a sneaky little move in which you hit your approach putt and then quickly walk up and rake up what's left of it, no matter the length, before your opponents can stop you or think to holler, "Hey, wait a minute!" Trump has mastered this move. He does it sometimes before the ball has even stopped rolling. MSNBC cameras caught him doing it once to a ball that had sped five feet past the hole and was gaining speed. By the time anybody can object, the ball is already in his pocket.

*The Ball Switch

"Whenever I've caddied in Trump's group," says Puga, "he always gets his own cart. He makes sure to hit first off every tee box and then jumps in the cart, so he's halfway down the fairway before the other three are done driving. That way he can get up there quick and mess with his ball. So this one time—we were on the 18th—he hits first, kind of blocks it right, and jumps in his cart and starts driving away. My guy pures one right down the middle. I mean, I SAW it go right down the middle. One of his best drives of the day. But by the time we get to my guy's ball, it's not there. We can't find it anywhere. And Trump is now ON the green already putting! Where's our ball? And then Trump starts yelling back at us, "Hey guys! I made a birdie!" He's holding up his ball and celebrating. And that's when we realized. That fucker stole our ball! He got up here early, hit OUR ball, and then hurried up and pretended like he made the putt for a birdie. I mean, what the hell?"

Once, Trump played a course with one of L.A.'s more famous holes—a par 5 where Howard Hughes once landed his plane to pick up Katherine Hepburn for a date—that has a pond just left of the green. "I saw Trump's ball go in the lake," one of the caddies told me. "I mean, I saw the ripples! But by the time we caught up to him and his cart, the ball was back on the fairway. When we asked him what happened, he said, 'Must've been the tide.'"

Proof Trump cheats is that whenever he plays in front of TV cameras, he goes from hero to hack.

The famous Pebble Beach Pro-Am is a four-day, three-course pro-celebrity clam bake started by Bing Crosby and televised yearly by CBS. This is the one Bill Murray always enters. At the Pebble event, there are really two tournaments going on—the pro one and the team one. Each tournament has a separate cut.

In the team one, you make the cut as a team—you and your pro—but Trump's team never did. He played in it seven times and never made the cut. The closest he came was in 1998 when the whole thing was cancelled for weather. You might say, "Well, there you have it. Trump had terrible pro partners."

TRUMP SCORES IN TELEVISED TOURNAMENTS

AT&T Pebble Beach Pro-Am (Pebble Beach, CA)

Year	Trump's Pro	Team Finish	Pro Finish
1993	Paul Goydos	Missed Cut	Missed Cut
1998	Fulton Allem	Weather Cancellation	Tie 45th
2001	Jim McGovern	Missed Cut	Tie 63rd
2002	Brad Elder	Missed Cut	Missed Cut
2003	Brian Claar	Missed Cut	Tie 42nd
2005	David Frost	Missed Cut	Missed Cut
2006	John Cook	Missed Cut	Tie 53rd

American Century Celebrity Championship (Lake Tahoe, NV)

Year	Finish	Score	# of Players	Winner	Winning Score
2004	56th	–12*	80	Dan Quinn (hockey)	74*
2005	42nd	26*	80	Billy Joe Tolliver (football)	76*
2006	62nd	268	80	Jack Wagner (actor)	213

*Stableford point system.

Not true. His pro partners for those seven years were solid Tour players—Paul Goydos, Fulton Allem, Jim McGovern, Brad Elder, Brian Claar, David Frost, and John Cook. But in the six tourneys that finished, Trump's pro went on to make the pro cut four times. Take a typical year, 2006: The Cook/Trump team finished 111th, but Cook made the pro cut. The weak link was Trump.

The other true measure of Trump's golf game was the American Century Celebrity Championship at Lake Tahoe, a woodsy course on the California-Nevada border. Tahoe gets a stellar, raucous field of celebs most years—ex-athletes, actors, singers, scratch players, and duffers. Trump played the Tahoe event three times—2004, 2005, and 2006.

In those three Tahoe tries, he never finished in the top half of the field. The first year, he was 56th out of 80, which is not stellar when you consider the field includes players like the famously golf-plagued Charles Barkley. The next time, he finished 42nd out of 80. Finally, in that calamitous 2006 Tahoe tournament, he finished 62nd out of 80 and averaged 89.3 per round, and that's with Tahoe's rule that no player can take worse than a double bogey. Then again, Trump may have been exhausted. According to lawsuits raging as this book went to press, he had affairs with two different women at that one single tournament—porn star Stormy Daniels and *Playboy* model Karen McDougal.

So, just to recap, in those three Tahoe tries alone, the man who once said, "When it comes to golf, there are very few people who can beat me," was beaten by 157 people, or more than 60% of those who tried.

*   *   *

So how is Clinton's cheating different than Trump's?

It isn't. It's still cheating. But Clinton's methods were less diabolical and more goofy. Trump's are often so over-the-top it verges on sad. Clinton wasn't trying to pretend he was six shots better than he really was. With Trump, the cheating was a path to something more important: I win again. With Clinton, the cheating was more like, "Doggone it. I know I can do this! Let me try again." (And again. And again.) It's like the difference between a guy who goes to the bank and steals the pen versus the guy who steals the vault.

Trump's friends defend his cheating, but in a way you might not expect. "My rounds with him have been some of the most fun days I've ever had playing golf," says Coach Dunleavy. "Yeah, he moves it and kicks it and all that, but no money changes hands at the end. There's a wager, yeah, but then nobody pays anybody. So that's not really cheating to me. It's just fun."

To show how much fun, Dunleavy tells a story about he and Trump as partners in a game against two of their buddies. Dunleavy hits his approach shot onto the corner of a kidney-shaped green that left him no possible putt. He was going to have to chip it off the green or somehow try to putt through the fringe and hope it came out back onto the green. Trump, his partner, came over and secretly knocked the ball on to a part of the green where Dunleavy could putt it. Dunleavy picked it up and put it back where it was.

"That's when Donald starts yelling to the other two," Dunleavy recalls. "He goes, 'Guys, guys! I wanna tell you how great a guy Coach is. I knocked his ball over here so he could have a putt at it. But then he put it back! And that's why he's an unemployed coach and I'm worth $13 billion."

5

BUY, LIE, AND CRY

Owning a great golf course gives you great power.
—DONALD J. TRUMP

ONE CHRISTMAS, WHEN DONALD Trump was small, he and his younger brother Robert got building blocks. The next day, Donald asked Robert if he could borrow his blocks to build something big. His brother was happy to lend them. Donald used the blocks to build a huge building that almost reached the ceiling.

"He was so proud of it," his late mother recalled. The next day, Robert asked for his blocks back. But Donald couldn't do it. He'd glued them all together.

If Donald Trump could glue together every great golf course in the world and slap his name on them, he would. But he doesn't. Instead, he takes the ones he owns and *pretends* they're the best. As of late 2018, he owned 14 golf courses and operated or will operate another five. The Trump name is on golf courses in America, the UAE, Scotland, Ireland, and, soon, Indonesia.

Trump Golf Courses and Golf Resorts

America

Course	Location	Access
Trump National Golf Club, Westchester	Briarcliff Manor, NY	private
Trump National Golf Club, Bedminster, NJ	Bedminster Township, NJ	private
Trump National Golf Club Hudson Valley	Hopewell Junction, NY	private
Trump National Golf Club Philadelphia	Pine Hill, NJ	private
Trump National Golf Club Colts Neck	Colts Neck, NJ	private
*Trump Golf Links at Ferry Point	New York City, the Bronx	public
Trump National Golf Club Washington, D.C.	Sterling, VA	private
Trump National Doral Golf Club	Miami, FL	public
Trump National Golf Club Jupiter	Jupiter, FL	private
Trump International Golf Club	West Palm Beach, FL	private
Trump National Golf Club Charlotte	Mooresville, NC	private
Trump National Golf Club Los Angeles	Rancho Palos Verdes, CA	public

Overseas

Course	Location	Access
Trump International Golf Links, Aberdeen	Balmedie, Scotland	public
Trump Turnberry	Ayrshire, Scotland	public
Trump International Golf Links & Hotel	Doonbeg, Ireland	public
*Trump International Golf Club, Dubai	Dubai, UAE	public
*Trump World Golf Club	Dubai, UAE	public

In Development

Course	Location
*Trump International Golf Club & Resort	Bali (Indonesia)
*Lido City	Indonesia

*Operates only.

"Somebody made the statement that Donald Trump has built or owns the greatest collection of golf courses, ever, in the history of golf," Trump once said. "And I believe that is 100% true."

Would that somebody be Trump? Because nobody who knows golf would say that. His lineup of courses is nice, but since he always buys properties that are in default or bankrupt at, as he often says, "10 or 15 cents on the dollar," he's often trying to put rouge on a cadaver. One he bought—Trump Los Angeles—had just fallen into the Pacific. He does not have a single course in the 2019–2020 *Golf Digest's* Top 100 American courses, the bible of all golf rankings. In fact, he doesn't have a single course in the top 175. The best he can do is Trump International in West Palm Beach (178). He does much better overseas, though. Of the three courses he owns in Europe, two are on *Golf Digest's* Top 100 World (outside the U.S.) list: Trump Turnberry (10) and Trump International at Aberdeen (64).

His other courses—Trump Los Angeles (CA), Trump Washington (VA), National Hudson (NY), Trump Colts Neck (NY), Trump Philadelphia (NJ), Trump Charlotte (NC), Trump Ferry Links (the Bronx), Trump Doral (FL), Trump Jupiter (FL), and Doonbeg in Ireland—are all bologna sandwiches on white bread. They'll fill you with golf for the day, but you'll never salivate about them later.

So that isn't "the greatest collection of golf courses ever, in the history of golf." It's not even the best collection owned by any American now. That would be Trump's rival, Chicago greeting-card tycoon Mike Keiser, who owns Bandon Dunes resort in Oregon. All four of his courses there are in the Top 100 American list. Keiser also owns Cabot Cliffs in Nova Scotia (9), Barnbougle Dunes in Tasmania (11), and Barnbougle Lost Farm in Australia (23). So the Top 100 list score would be Keiser 7, Trump 2. Although Trump has gotten one bite of revenge: Keiser backed Jeb Bush for president.

But one thing is true of all of Trump's courses: the attention to detail is immaculate. Everything must be perfect. The man will spend an hour looking at every green on *the practice range*. The problem is that golf is not a game of perfect. It's meant to be like nature, played over stream and stones. That's what makes it better than tennis. Every golf course is different and new and you never know what kind of lie you're going to get. But Trump golf is stuffy, all too combed and primped, with way too many cart paths and waterfalls and fairways your Foot Joys sink into. Trump doesn't build golf courses so much as financial statements.

Trump's first course was Trump International Golf Club in West Palm Beach, Florida, an 11-minute drive from his Mar-a-Lago social club and hotel. He built the course in 1999 from scratch. He might have given it such a $50 name because it was such a 50-cent piece of property. It was 300 grungy acres of weedy vacant lots, surrounded on one side by the county jail, on the other by the airport, on another by a string of bail bonds houses and immigration passport/visa joints, and on the final side by a strip joint.

How Trump got Trump International in the first place was pure Trumpaliciousness. It started with the purchase of Mar-a-Lago Club, the gold-dripping mansion Trump bought in 1985. He began complaining that the jets at nearby Palm Beach International Airport were making too much noise over his bedroom. Very unfair. But was that new? Did planes suddenly start diverting over Mar-a-Lago just to spite Trump? Nope. Nothing had changed much in the flight paths for 60 years. In fact, Mar-a-Lago has had a red flashing light on top of it as far back as anybody can remember. Didn't matter to Trump. It was violating his sensitive ears. He sued.

The first suit went nowhere. Undaunted, he sued then-airport director Bruce Pelley, personally, three times. One time he sued him for assault, complaining that it was as if Pelley were "standing in front of Mar-a-Lago with a noise gun." The court didn't buy it. Trump even sued Pelley for fraud, saying that Pelley was purposely sending airplanes to get even with him. Pelley, of course, didn't control the path of the airplanes. That was done by the FAA and the tower. All three suits died slow deaths.

The truth is Trump wasn't really after peace and solitude. He was after the scrubby wasteland *next* to the airport. He was hoping one of the lawsuits would go through and he could get that land in a settlement to build a golf course for his swanky Mar-a-Lago crowd to play. It didn't work, but when he was out of lawsuits, he pitched the West Palm Beach County Commissioners the idea of him leasing the land anyway. What good was it doing them? They struck a deal.

(Note: Despite what you see in articles over and over again, Trump did not "win the land in a settlement." That's what he told reporters once he signed the lease, but it's a lie. "Absolutely not true," says one Palm Beach official who didn't want to be identified because...well...you know. "His noise lawsuits went nowhere. This was a business deal, pure and simple. But as soon as he signed the lease, he went to the *Palm Beach Post* and told them he'd won it in a settlement. They wrote it, and it keeps getting repeated over and over.")

But why would the county want to get in bed with a guy who'd sued them so many times? Because Trump could charm an elephant into doing an arabesque. Just to protect themselves, the county included a clause: Trump could never sue them again. (He would anyway.)

Trump poured millions into that flat-as-a-tortilla land. To

make a course that he promised would be "the best in America," there was only one architect to hire: Tom Fazio. Fazio not only built Steve Wynn's Shadow Creek in Las Vegas, a course Trump lusted after for its majestic fake waterfall, but Fazio has landed more courses on *Golf Digest*'s Top 100 list than any living American architect. Trump had to have Tom Fazio.

But Fazio was too expensive, so Trump hired his brother, Jim Fazio. This is a little like wanting Michael Jackson to play at your bar mitzvah but getting Tito instead. At Trump's order, Jim put in massive dunes where there were no dunes, a 75-foot-high 18th tee box, and a faux waterfall big enough to turn Steve Wynn green. He sodded it with lush grass and posted 889 canary date palms around the perimeter. He bathed his clubhouse interior in gold and put the whole thing behind big, black, screw-you gilded gates that screamed "Keep Out"—even though the whole place was set on leased public land.

Now all he had to do was talk Trump International up. Nobody on earth better at that. His course was going to be "the best course anywhere in America," he said. It was going to be "incredible" and "amazing," and there was "going to be nothing like it in the world." And it *was* pretty good, if your taste runs to fake Eiffel Towers in front of your hotel. But it's like a woman who's late to the beauty stylist. After a while, you just can't hide your roots. Unseemly things kept happening.

Take, for instance, the Palm Beach County Jail, which stands nine stories high and looms over one of the holes. In the first couple of years the course opened, the exercise yard was on one of the higher floors, so inmates would climb up the fencing and yell awful things at the well-heeled players. "It used to be you went past there and the guys in the exercise yard could see you," says a man who played there often as a guest. "And man, they'd get on you. 'Hey, white boy! You come in here and I'd have you for lunch!'" As author and member James Patterson likes to say, "Little criminals up there, big criminals down here."

Then there was the infamous Black Swan Murder. In 2001, a man named Cyril Wagner—the guest of a Palm Beach doctor—was playing the 17th when a big black swan known as "Alex" came at him with menace. Mr. Wagner swung an iron at it. Alex didn't duck and was struck dead. Wagner said it was the swan or him, self-defense. Trump banned Mr. Wagner forever. "But I probably sold 20 memberships out of that," Trump told me. *Man, you talk about lucky!*

Then there was the topper, the night in April 2018 when the strip joint that sits on the corner of this seedy area, Ultra, hosted none other than porn star Stormy Daniels. As part of her "Make America Horny Again" tour, Ms. Daniels stormed Ultra, dancing to Tom Petty's "American Girl" and coming undressed as Wonder Woman. She performed to a sardined house, some of whom paid as much as $1,000 to see her, all within a 9-iron of Trump's golf club. It's unclear whether Trump International members got a discount.

The president wasn't there, but almost everybody else was. People stopped their cars in the parking lot just to get their picture taken in front of the marquee. The parking lot was jammed with limos and pickups, the kind of event that could unite both sides of the aisle.

"I'd pay $35 to see what the big guy got his hands on," one limo driver said. One gentleman said he was only there to "support the First Amendment."

A true patriot.

Ready for a little quiz?

Okay...

1. Trump National Golf Club Washington, D.C., is in what city? (Hint: It's not Washington.)
2. Trump National Golf Club Los Angeles is where? (Hint: It's not Los Angeles.)
3. Trump National Golf Club Charlotte is in what town? (Hint: It's not Charlotte.)
4. Where is Trump National Golf Club Philadelphia located? (Hint: It's not even in Pennsylvania.)
5. What's so international about Trump International Golf Club West Palm Beach? (Hint: Not much.)

Answers:

1. Trump Washington is in Sterling, Virginia, a 45-minute drive from the White House.
2. Trump Los Angeles is in Rancho Palos Verdes, California, 75 minutes south of L.A.
3. Trump Charlotte is in Mooresville, North Carolina, an hour from Charlotte.

4. Trump Philadelphia is in Pine Hill, New Jersey, about 45 minutes from Philly.

5. Trump International is in West Palm Beach, Florida, which isn't very international at all. The vast majority of members are American citizens.

And if that little subterfuge bothers you, you haven't seen anything yet.

Trump's m.o. when he buys a golf course is always the same: Buy, Lie, and Cry.

Buy: Trump always buys at the bottom. He gets deals, whether it's a decrepit hotel, abandoned land, or a golf course that's gone bust. Then he pours money into it, just never as much as he says. Whenever you hear Trump talk about how much money he poured into a golf course—"$200 million" "$250 million"—you can divide that at least by 10. Then he slaps his name on it and begins to...

Lie: Because Trump is the greatest press wrangler in American business history, he immediately begins talking up his courses so big you'd think he'd just put 18 holes inside the Taj Mahal. Every course is set "on the greatest piece of property anyone's ever seen. And that's not me saying that." (Yes, it's usually just him saying that.) Every course is "way better" than (insert name of famous course in the same state). "And that's guys at (insert same course name here) telling me that." He needs to talk it up so he can convince people to pay $200,000 to join a course that two years before was a goat track.

Now it's time to...

Cry: At the very same time he's telling the world how awesome his piece of property is, he's suing the cities they're in for overvaluing it.

Take Trump Westchester (NY), his second course. Trump bought it in 1996 when it was a vanilla sort of course known as Briar Hall Golf and Country Club in Ossining, New York. It was owned by the bank, which sold it to him for $7.5 million. Trump immediately bulldozed it and put Fazio the Lesser on it. He built a typically immaculate and overwrought course—the waterfall on No. 13 is over 101 feet high and is so fake looking you're sure you saw it on *Fantasy Island*. Trump started talking it up like it was the greatest thing since the Vardon grip. "This will be the best course in New York," he crowed, fully aware that New York has Shinnecock, Friar's Head, and a dozen other showstoppers. He signed up celebs—for free, of course—Yankees skipper Joe Torre, Jack Nicholson, and Hugh Grant. Trump even gave Bill Clinton a freebie. It was a hit.

On his financial-disclosure declaration during the presidential campaign, he valued it at $50 million. In fact, he valued ALL of his golf courses at $50 million, for a whopping total of $700 million. That's a statement that belongs in a padded room. No way. Never. Fifty million for a golf course like Trump West Palm Beach with no hotel and no land to build homes on? Preposterous. The golf world howled at that canard.

"I've evaluated over 3,500 courses in America, Canada, the Caribbean, all over," says Larry Hirsh, a golf course value analyst for Golf Property Analysts near Philadelphia. "And I can only recall one property that we appraised anywhere near $50 million."

Which course?

"I can't say. But it was a very well-known multi-course golf resort that most every American golfer knows. It has more than two courses, I can tell you that."

Was it a Trump course?

"No."

(My guess: It's got to be Pebble Beach, Pinehurst, or Bandon Dunes.)

What's the most expensive 18-holes-only course you've ever evaluated?

"Somewhere in the $20 millions," Hirsh said.

Okay, so Trump's $50 million value for each of his courses is just a flat-out Double Whopper with extra cheese. But get this: At the same time Trump was saying Westchester was worth $50 million, he was suing Ossining for its $11 million tax valuation of it. His lawyer said that was way too high. Trump insisted it was only worth $1.4 million. That's a $48 million difference, if you're scoring at home.

Says Patterson, "I'll give him $1.6 million for it right now."

With two under his belt, Trump started thinking even bigger. He bought the 450-acre Bedminster, New Jersey, hunting and horse estate of the former car tycoon John DeLorean, whose *Back to the Future* car company had gone belly up and who had personally gone broke in a cocaine scandal. Trump got it for a song—$35 million. Trump started interviewing course designers, but this time with a twist.

He started with one of America's best golf designers, Bobby Jones, Jr., the son of the legendary architect Robert Trent Jones. Jones is from New Jersey, so it piqued his interest. But when he sat down in Trump's office for the interview, Trump had a surprise.

"You'll design and build the course, but your name won't be on it," Trump said.

Jones had to blink a few times.

"Excuse me?" he said. "Whose name will be on it?"

"Mine."

More blinking.

"Wait. You want me to ghostwrite your golf course?"

"Yes. Exactly."

Jones passed. Trump got Fazio instead, the real one this time, Tom. Turns out Fazio loves Trump. "He's just so much fun," Fazio says. "I love the guy. He's crazy. He's nonstop. He has so much energy. He's so funny and he never stops. The guy never sleeps. He calls you at all hours. Good thing he doesn't drink. Can you imagine all that on booze? Oh man."

Fazio took the job, but only if his name *was* on it. Even then, he had his regrets. "Donald would constantly chopper out (from New York City), wanting to talk details. Details, details, so many details. So, finally, my son just moved onto the grounds for the entire project. No way I was going to deal with Donald every single day. Besides, I don't work weekends and the guy never stops working."

Eventually, Tom stopped working for Trump and stuck to just being friends. "He uses Jim," Fazio says. "He does good work and he's much cheaper. And it doesn't matter to Donald. He just tells people, 'This is by Tom Fazio' anyway."

Bedminster—which now has 36 holes—is also a hit. It's already held a woman's major, the 2017 U.S. Women's Open, and will hold the 2022 PGA Championship.

After Bedminster, Trump went on a buying spree. In 2002, he bought the partially ocean-swallowed Ocean Trails in Rancho Palos Verdes and called it Trump National Golf Club Los Angeles. In 2009, he bought a course in Pine Hill, New Jersey, and called it Trump Philadelphia. He bought a course called Branton Woods in New York and called it Trump National Golf Club Hudson Valley. That was an adventure in itself.

The contact point for the sale was longtime golf executive Ian Gillule, who was working for the seller, Eric Bergstol. Gillule got Trump interested in the course, and Trump suggested they go up and see it that Saturday. But that wasn't going to work for Bergstol. "No, no, no, definitely not Saturday," Bergstol said. "I have to be discreet. We're having a member–member (tournament) on Saturday. None of the members know I'm selling it. Tell him Monday. We're closed Monday. He'll have the whole place to himself."

Trump wasn't budging. "I'll never forget what he said on the phone that day," Gillule remembers. "He said, 'You tell Eric that on weekends I make million-dollar deals. On weekdays, I make *billion-dollar* deals. You tell him I'll be there Saturday, but I'll be discreet. Nobody will know I'm there.'"

"Discreet" and "Trump" go together like "gasoline" and "soup." Trump and Gillule drove from Manhattan up to Hudson Valley in Trump's white Rolls-Royce. "As we pull up, I see that the carts are all staged, dozens and dozens of them, all in a row," Gillule recalls. "All the players are gathered there and the pro is giving everybody instructions. And it was literally like Rodney Dangerfield showing up in *Caddyshack*. He pulls that big white Rolls-Royce right up on the curb in front, gets out, and yells, 'Hey everybody! How you doing? I'm buying this place!'"

In 2012, Trump bought the former The Point Lake and called it Trump National Golf Club Charlotte. Trump made a ton of changes on that one, not all of which pleased the course's original designer, the golfing legend Greg Norman. Trump was playing with Norman and two writers and Norman seemed pissed the whole round, they say. Might have been because Trump told Norman he wouldn't change anything, and on the first three holes they played, Norman saw that he'd changed something on *every hole*. He was frying. He'd hit his shot, get back in the cart, glare at Trump, and speak to nobody. Trump came over to *Golf Digest*'s Jaime Diaz and said, "Greg is behaving very poorly. He should be better. The fans should be entertained by him."

If you think Norman was pissed that day, you should hear him talk about what Trump did to one of his next purchases—Doonbeg in Ireland.

"That was my favorite course I ever built by hand," Norman

remembers. (A "by-hand" golf course is one that is built almost entirely without bulldozers or tractors, one that threads itself through the natural landscape without moving much earth.) "It was just my baby. We worked with the environmentalists, hand in glove, to build a course that they wanted, the developer wanted, and the community wanted. It was my passion, my labor of love."

Trump bought it, kept the clubhouse, and practically redid the entire course. Most Irish golf critics have panned the Trump version. "Usually, there's an unwritten code," Norman says. "You call the architect and talk over any changes. But, not in this case, I guess....To have somebody else come in and change it all around, that really bothered me. So I just switched off. I haven't gone back. I don't want to go back. I'll never go back."

When an architect agrees to work for Trump, he needs to understand the "for" part. It's Trump's course and he'll get it the way he wants, even if it makes no sense. You just draw it up. "He's the boss," Tom Fazio says. "What are you gonna do? He writes the checks."

But here's the crazy thing: Trump is actually a pretty good golf architect. At his 36-hole Trump Washington, he worked nothing short of a miracle, without Fazio's input, stealing holes from the lesser 18, rerouting the course to better showcase the Potomac River, and building a couple world-class par 3s. "It's a much, much better facility than it was prior to him buying it," says member Gary Newman. "And it was all him doing the work."

So if Trump was the architect for Trump Washington, did

Trump stiff Trump? Because he's famous for short-changing architects. One prominent American architect refuses to work for him. "He called me about doing a course, so I asked around. All the references I got were the same. He does a lot of jerking you around, trying to sucker you."

Architect Gil Hanse has worked a lot with Trump. Not long ago, though, Hanse got up at a corporate dinner, gave his speech, and then said, "I'll take any questions you have, except ones about Donald Trump."

It's not so much the promises Trump breaks or the lies he tells, it's the sheer volume of them. For three years, freelance documentary maker Matt Howley and his crew followed Trump everywhere for Golf Channel's *Donald J. Trump's Fabulous World of Golf.* The idea was to showcase Trump's burgeoning golf-course empire. They had *carte blanche* access to Trump, who loved the attention. It meant more sizzle, and more sizzle means more members, and more members means more initiation fees in his pocket.

"Donald Trump really treated us well," Howley says. "He was great. He knew everybody's name, asked a million questions. He was very kind."

There was only one problem. "I was always introduced as the president of the Golf Channel," Howley says with a laugh. "One time, he introduced me as the president of Golf Channel and this whole Japanese table of businessmen got up and bowed to me. I didn't know what to do, so I bowed back."

If Howley wasn't the president of Golf Channel, then he and his crew were suddenly from *60 Minutes*, especially if they were walking through the dining room at Mar-a-Lago. "He'd go from table to table, shaking people's hands and saying, 'Yeah, *60 Minutes* is with me.'"

Why wasn't the truth good enough? Why wasn't, "This is a crew from Golf Channel. They're documenting me for my show," impressive enough for Trump?

"Because that's his gold standard for TV—*60 Minutes*," Howley says. "He always goes for his gold standard. I got used to it. After a while, I started to *believe* I was with *60 Minutes*. Honestly, just from spending so much time around him, I found myself lying much more than I used to. My friends started getting on me about it. They'd be like, 'Dude, that didn't happen that way. Why are you lying about it?' You tell enough lies and you sort of forget after a while."

When you toss that much bullshit around, it's hard to remember where the piles are. For instance, Trump once said of the former Lowes Island Club he turned into Trump Washington, "This place, when it's finished, will be the finest club anywhere in the country. There will be nothing like it."

But, wait. That's almost exactly what he said about Trump Los Angeles when it opened: "No one has ever seen anything like this. There is nothing that you can compare it to.... It's going to be the greatest, most spectacular golf course that you've ever seen."

But that can't be, because that's almost exactly what he said about Trump Jupiter: "It doesn't get any finer."

But how can that be when he promised Trump Doral would be "the finest resort and golf club in the country"?

Now you're completely confused, because he declared Trump Turnberry to be, "The greatest golf course anywhere in the world. Everybody knows it."

Speaking of manure, Trump also says, repeatedly, "I've been given more golf environmentalism awards than anybody." That's the Moby Dick of fibs. He hasn't been given one legitimate golf environmental award. Not one. Zero.

He is proud of the great numbers of people he employs at his golf properties, but, as ever, those numbers get the Trump Bump. "I employ thousands of people," he told Golf Channel's David Feherty. "I take care of their kids' educations ... [pause] ... well, indirectly."

Wait, indirectly?

If that's true, can Trump say he fights fires because some of his taxes go to the fire department? Does he save people's lives because the city hospital gets subsidized?

Sometimes the gap between the truth and the Trumps is so great you couldn't cross it with a Cessna. Take Trump Golf Links at Ferry Point in the Bronx, New York.

The Truth: In the early 1980s, the City of New York decided to build a golf course on a condemned garbage dump. They got Jack Nicklaus to design it and went through two or three developers trying to get it made. Finally, they gave up and did it themselves. By 2008, it was almost done. They hired the Trump Organization to operate it, as long as it agreed to build a $10 million clubhouse and handle the grow-in of the greens, which usually takes a year and a half. Sweet deal for Trump, who didn't have to pay the city a cent the first four years it was open. It finally did open in 2015—with 15-foot-high letters that read: TRUMP LINKS.

The Trump: "*That course would not have been open for 10 years more had I not gotten involved,*" *Trump told* Crain's New York Business. "*It wasn't getting built. Nobody could get it open....I was able to do it. I got it open.*" *Ivanka Trump even went so far as to blog that* "*My family was able to do in two years what the city hadn't been able to do in two decades....My father went out to the construction site, where he saw a bunch of guys literally moving sand from one end of the course to the other. He essentially looked at them and said, 'You guys have made a lot of money pushing sand around for the last 20 years, but that stops with me. It's time to get this done.' And they did.*"

The Truth: No. The course was almost done except for the greens, a few cart paths, and a couple lightning shelters. Adrian Benepe, who was the NYC parks commissioner at the time, still shudders about it. "That was the first time I realized the whole family was pathological liars," Benepe says. "Ivanka just made her story up. Just invented it. He didn't bring that course in. We finished it."

The Trump: When Trump became POTUS, his son Eric became the mouthpiece for all the golf properties, and a new generation of fable telling began. Ten years after Trump signed on, they finally opened the clubhouse. (Although it wasn't really ready to open. They did it to coincide with the 2018 U.S. Open on Long Island.) Eric came to the ribbon-cutting ceremony and said, "You literally cannot get on the course, it's so packed."

The Truth: It definitely is *not* hard to get on Ferry Point. On June 30, 2018—a Saturday—I went to their website to book a tee time for the next morning. A Sunday summer morning tee time in New York, on a course that's "packed"? That would be hard, right? All they had left for a foursome was 9:40 a.m., 11:30, 11:40, 11:50, noon, 12:10 p.m., 12:30, 12:40, 12:50, 1:00, 1:10, 1:20, 1:40, 2:00, 2:10, 2:20, 2:40, 2:50, 3:00, 3:10...you get the idea.

The Trump: Eric Trump said business at Ferry Point is "spectacular."

The Truth: Business is not spectacular. In 2016, gross receipts were down 9% from 2015. In 2017, they were down 17% from 2016. That's been true across all of golf, but it's particularly grating when a city is trying to make back the whopping $127 million it sunk into a course.

The Trump: Eric and Ivanka speak of Ferry Point as some kind of city-beautification project that the family sacrificed to build, out of their civic hearts, like they ought to be on a United Way poster.

The Truth: The Trumps have been paid and paid well for operating the place. As for brightening the lives of Bronx golfers, they haven't. At $175 a round for a resident, almost nobody from the Bronx can play it. The patrons are mostly Wall Street guys and midtown execs and Yankees pitchers with the day off. By far, the biggest winners in the deal have been the Trumps.

The Trump: When it opened, Trump tweeted:

TrumpGolf Links at Ferry Point will host many major championships over the years. Great thing for NYC— congratulations to all!

The Truth: It has yet to have one.

6

THE GREAT MUCKLE GYPE

I think his mother would be horrified.

—MAIRI STERLAND, TRUMP'S COUSIN

IN SCOTLAND, DONALD TRUMP is less popular than tipping. They hated him before he was president, and now they hate him more than the English. They don't hide it. I saw one guy who held up a giant sign that read: "Keep Scotland Great—Get Trump Out."

Since I speak a little Scottish, allow me to translate a few others:

- Trump You Great Muckle Gype! (Trump You Big Lumpy Fool!)
- Trump You Tangerine Roaster! (Trump You Orange Idiot!)
- Clackwanker! (Douche!)
- You Weapons-Grade Wanker! (You Very Large Jagoff!)
- Trump Is a Witless Cocksplat! (Trump Is a Dummy Head!)

- Trump You Clueless Numpty! (Trump You Stupid Know-Nothing!)
- You Wankmaggot! (Doesn't translate.)
- What a Gobshite! (What a Useless Prick!)
- Trump You Orange Bawbag! (Trump You Orange Testicle Sack!)
- Get Out, King Fucktwaddle (Self-explanatory.)

That's a lot of animus for a guy whose mother was *born* in Scotland. If anybody else with a Scottish-born mother had been elected U.S. president, Scotland might have given him Dundee and half of Edinburgh. "It's hard to put into words how big that would be here," says John Huggan, the longtime Scottish golf writer. "A half-Scottish president? Oh my god. But now it's just completely the opposite. He is genuinely hated here. I haven't met anybody who wants him here. He's an arse. He's the walking caricature of what some Scots think Americans are like—loud, brash, and obnoxious."

Among the things they hate about him is that everything he seems to know about the UK you could fit on the head of a golf tee. For instance, Trump owns a golf course in Ireland called Doonbeg. At the press conference Trump held before his July 2018 trip to the British Isles, a reporter asked Trump if he was worried about the high level of venom the UK spits his way. "I believe the people in the UK—Scotland, Ireland, I have property in Ireland, as you know—those people they like me a lot." The only problem with that answer is that Ireland isn't in the UK. That's Northern Ireland.

His White House staff doesn't seem to know where Scotland is, either. As he was leaving England to go visit his Trump Turnberry golf resort on the west coast of Scotland, the official White House Twitter page announced:

Today, @realDonaldTrump and @FLOTUS had tea with Her Majesty Queen Elizabeth II at Windsor Castle before departing the UK.

The only problem with that tweet is that Turnberry is very much in the UK, as is Scotland, come to think of it.

On June 24, 2016—the day after the UK's Brexit vote—Trump happened to be in Turnberry. He tweeted:

Just arrived in Scotland. Place is going wild over the vote. They took their country back, just like we will take America back.

The only problem with that tweet is that Scotland voted 62% *against* Brexit.

He then went to a raucous ribbon-cutting press conference, set in front of the Turnberry lighthouse, escorted by bagpipers in kilts and was confronted by a comedian who threw Nazi-logo golf balls at him.

It got worse. He returned home and started telling reporters that he'd predicted Brexit. "I was in Turnberry the day before," he said more than a few times. "I saw it coming." The only problem with that is he was there the day *after*, and every UK newspaper has proof.

Then, somehow, it got worse than that. On his 2018 UK visit, Double Down doubled down. "I predicted Brexit," he told the *Sun* newspaper of London. "I was cutting a ribbon for the opening of Turnberry—you know they totally did a whole renovation, it is beautiful—the day before the Brexit vote...I said, 'Brexit will happen.' The vote is going to go positive, because people don't want to be faced with the horrible immigration problems." Then he REPEATED it.

Finally, just to add a little seasoning to the whole bouillabaisse of naked lies, bonehead errors, and cultural insults, Trump said, "You know, my mother is from here. I'm Scotch."

The only problem with that is nobody's "Scotch." They're Scottish.

Blue-eyed Maryanne MacLeod was born on the Isle of Lewis, about as far north in Scotland as you can go, in a tiny town called Tong, near Stornoway, youngest of 10 children of peasant parents. In 1930, at age 17, she boarded the ship *Transylvania* out of Glasgow, bound for New York, to live with a sister. All but one of her siblings would do the same—chain migration, as Trump calls it. She worked as a maid until she happened to meet a rich German-born New York apartment tycoon name Fred Trump and married him in 1936.

But what kind of story is that? Young Donald Trump went to work making it sound better. "She was on vacation in America when she met my dad," he tells people.

Trump's mother had five kids—Maryanne, Frederick Jr.,

Elizabeth, Donald, and Robert—and returned to Tong every year, still speaking fluent Scottish Gaelic despite her fancy Bloomingdale's dresses. She returned every year until late into the 1990s, but Donald only went with her once, as a toddler, and never went again. Maybe it's what the Scottish wind does to that hairdo, which makes it look like a snapping red wolverine.

Never went again, that is, until 2006, when he wanted to build a luxury public golf resort near Balmedie, just north of Aberdeen on the east coast. For $11 million, he'd purchased an old shooting ranch called the Menie Estate, perched on a delicate stretch of dunes land designated SSSI—Site of Special Scientific Interest— Scotland's most sensitive grade. Environmental groups were breathless with anger over the idea. They pointed out, over and over, how much damage building a golf course could do to the giant, fragile, constantly moving dunes, much less Trump's two courses, not to mention an eight-story, five-star, 450-room hotel, a sports complex, 950 time-share apartments, and 36 villas. Made no difference to Trump. He wanted it, and he was going to get it.

So the day before he was to plead his case in front of the Aberdeenshire Council, he landed his jet in nearby Stornoway and visited his cousin, who still lives in the childhood home of his dear Scottish mother.

For 96 seconds.

He came up the walk, cameras clicking, waved a few times, went into the house, looked around, and came briskly out. Then he held a press conference that was two hours, or 75 times longer than the visit, mentioning more than once that he was "Scotch" and he was going to build "the greatest golf course in the world" and that he would create 6,000 jobs and bring $1.2 billion to the local economy. That figure, of course, was flubberdeegook. He'd started with $300 million and lathered his way up as he went.

Later, a Trump cousin, Mairi Sterland, told a Scottish blogger: "I used to laugh about [being related to] Donald Trump. Now I hardly dare mention him....He is outrageous. You quail at the thought of what he's capable of."

The "Hey, I'm Scotch, too" gambit didn't work. In November 2007, the council turned him down.

No problem. Trump went over their heads. He started wining and dining the head of the nation, Scotland First Minister Alex Salmond, a pro-business stalwart. "Salmond believed Trump's crap," says Suzanne Kelly, a reporter for the *Aberdeen Voice*. "He enjoyed flying back and forth to New York, eating Trump's steak and lobster dinners. He got the Trump mojo put on him." A year later, Salmond decided to override the environmentalists and the locals and the Aberdeenshire Council and grant Trump permission to build his golf resort, dunes be damned.

"Six thousand jobs across Scotland, 1,400 local and permanent jobs in the northeast of Scotland," Salmond reasoned. "That outweighs the environmental concerns."

Construction of the greatest course in the world was ready to start.

First thing Trump needed was an architect.

"First of all, he told me right away he never wanted to build any 36 holes," says American architect Tom Doak. "He told me, 'I asked for 36, hoping to get permitted for 18. All I wanted was the 18.' But then the Scottish government stepped in and gave him 36. 'And I don't even WANT 36!'" That was a problem for any architect to have to build an extra 18 boring "resort" holes and a problem for Trump to have to build them. "There were a ton of problems. I turned him down." Finally, on reportedly his fifth try, he got a respected English designer, Martin Hawtree.

Cue the bulldozers, accompanied by the screaming of the dunes huggers, who abhorred the flattening and pinning down of giant dunes that migrate 11 meters per year. In Scotland, moving dunes is akin to cementing over Walden Pond. Trump argued that by preventing sand movement he was "preserving the dunes." That's like saying a T-bone preserves the cow.

"That's a live dune system," says renowned Scottish designer David McLay Kidd. "When you stop them from moving, they're effectively dead."

Kidd would know. He was the last architect to build a golf course in an ultra-sensitive dunes site—the first to try in 100 years—in Machrihanish, which you drive to by taking Paul McCartney's long and winding road. They were so careful with the dunes, they might as well have been wearing oven mitts. "We used no heavy equipment at all," reports David Southworth, the American developer of the project. "Nothing. We did it with shovels, by hand. We couldn't disturb the orchids. We worked hand-in-hand with the environmentalists and the local people. It was a real challenge." What they gave them is a course called Machrihanish Dunes, which has been called "the most natural course on earth." What they gave him back is no protesters, no lawsuits, and no pissed-off locals.

Back to Trump. Reporters started digging in on the deal. Turns out, before Trump had shown official interest in the Menie Estate, he'd secretly tried to buy the neighboring houses and farms he thought were ugly, houses he didn't want his customers to have to look at. He sent his project director, Neil Hobday, knocking on doors, pretending to be an innocent passerby named "Peter White" (Hobday's middle names), inquiring cheerily if their homes were for sale. None were.

Would they want to sell them anyway, for a good price?

No, they wouldn't.

Trump bought the estate anyway and began brooding about those "ugly" houses.

Plan B: Trump had his lawyers apply to have the local government use eminent domain to buy the houses or, as they say in Scotland, "compulsory purchase." Didn't matter that this isn't at all how compulsory purchase works. It's meant for homes that are blighted, homes that stand in the way of a highway or a park. It's not a way for one neighbor to force out another because they don't like how his crabgrass looks. Again: Denied. (Trump's publicity people later claimed the "compulsory purchase" story was made up to build sympathy for the dunes residents. The only problem with that claim is that nearly every paper in Scotland has copies of Trump's application.)

Plan C: Start making life hell for the holdouts. Trump declared that one property, owned by a farmer named Michael Forbes, was a "slum" and that Forbes lived like a "pig." Then, just for seasoning, he added, "My mother was born in Stornoway. She was the most clean woman I've ever seen, immaculate. The people of Scotland are that way.... Maybe his heritage is from somewhere other than Scotland."

Forbes didn't go punch Trump and he didn't sue him. Instead, he put up a Mexican flag—in solidarity with other Trump insultees—and told Trump to "take his money and shove it up his arse." Not long after, Forbes and his elderly mother, Molly, who lives nearby, started having trouble with their water lines. She didn't sue, either. Instead, she just started trapping rain water in old paint buckets and getting water from a stream via wheelbarrow. She wouldn't move, either.

A neighbor named David Milne woke up one day to find that Trump had planted a row of giant trees blocking his 40-mile view of the coastline. He also found new 20-foot-high, 70-foot-long earth berms starting three feet from his property line, plus a new fence on two sides of his property, for which Trump sent him a $3,500 bill. Milne didn't sue. Instead, he threw away the bill, put up a Mexican flag, and waited for the trees to die. "Trump planted the wrong kind," Milne says. "Sitka spruces. Sitkas don't do well in our high winds and sea air." They did die. Trump's crews replaced those with more Sitkas, fronted by cypresses this time. "They'll die, too," Milne told me in July of 2018. "We can already see the sea through the gaps."

None of them moved. In fact, they moved others. They became local heroes. When a documentary came out about the whole mess—*You've Been Trumped*—they became national heroes. In fact, Michael Forbes was named "Scot of the Year" by Glenfiddich scotch. That fried Trump's brain. He immediately banned Glenfiddich from all his properties, tweeting...

Michael Forbes lives in a pigsty and bad liquor company Glenfiddich gave him Scot of the Year award....Does anyone smell publicity stunt?

...thus giving Glenfiddich more publicity than it could have ever dreamed.

It all amounted to a Scottish standoff. At press time, the second course still hadn't come, nor the hotel, nor the time-share condos, nor the 6,000 new jobs, nor the $1.28 billion for the economy. There was some talk about Trump trying again to build homes—500 of them—but when a Scotland Natural Heritage report came out in late summer 2018 showing that some of the dunes and much of the marine terraces had been damaged beyond repair, chances looked dismal for that, too.

"Donald Trump didn't do what he promised," admitted a sheepish Alex Salmond. "Balmedie got 10 cents on the dollar."

One golf course *was* built, though—Trump International Golf Links Scotland—and it's pretty good, if you like links courses that seemed to have been dreamed up by an interior designer. Links courses are supposed to be watered by the rain and cut by the wind. They're supposed to be a wrestling match between brown and green, with brown ahead on points. Bathed in wind, you play them along the ground, the kind of places where you putt from 100 yards out. Trump's course is much too lush, greener than the lawn of the Kentucky governor, so green it's blue-green. It doesn't thump. It swishes. Your feet sink.

The other problem is nobody plays it. I spent two days walking on it (under Scotland's Right to Roam laws) and never saw much of anybody—no Trump, no guards, and only one foursome each day. It was empty. For one, it's too expensive (almost $370 per round). For another, it's too Trump. "There might be people who would like to play it," says Martin Ford, an Aberdeenshire official who voted against the course, "but they don't want to give Trump their money."

Trump Aberdeen is a money pit. According to the required tax papers the club had to file, it lost $4.5 million in 2017. Remember those 6,000 people Trump was going to hire? It employed just 85 in 2017. Salmond now refers to Trump as "a complete and utter nincompoop."

"It was almost like the whole thing was a dry run for his campaign as president," Ford says. "He bullied everybody. He started false rumors. Established alternative truths by repetition. Then we watched the [presidential] campaign and it was everything he had done up here in Aberdeen."

It got worse. Trump found out 11 power-generating windmills were to be placed in the sea half a mile or so from his course and blew a gasket. He said they were so ugly they would spoil his guests' rounds of golf. Besides, he said, windmills are noisy, don't work, and kill birds. Salmond was a stone this time. Trump wrote more than a dozen letters to him excoriating him, threatening him, and begging him to kill the windmills. "Your country will become a third world wasteland that global investors will avoid," he wrote. Salmond didn't so much as wiggle a toe.

Trump sued. He lost. The windmills are churning out there now. You can't hear them, but you can see them from the beach, and he's right, they're not pretty. Of course, since you can't see the ocean much from his course, does it matter?

It did to Trump. "I doubt if I'll ever do business in Scotland again," he harrumphed.

Two years later, he bought another Scottish course.

In a land where you can't throw a bucket of birdseed without hitting a great golf course, Trump Turnberry stands out. Since Trump took over in 2014, it's twice as good as it was. When you throw in the magnificent par-5-length hotel that sits elegantly and high above it, it might be the best golf resort in the entire country. Nearly everything Trump botched in Aberdeen, he's done perfectly in Turnberry.

A true links course, Turnberry sits on the rocky site of Robert the Bruce's castle, guarded by a postcard white-and-yellow lighthouse where Robert Louis Stevenson roamed as a child (his dad was the keeper). Turnberry was just fine before Trump, of course. It delivered some of the greatest golf in history, including The Duel in the Sun in 1977 between Jack Nicklaus and Tom Watson. Turnberry is a beauty that's been unlucky in marriage. It's been owned by the Japanese, the Westin hotel chain, Arabs, just about everybody. "Trump is the first guy who's made promises to us and then actually delivered," says Clive Douglas, a former captain of the club. "He came in and bang, bang, bang. He did everything he said he'd do."

What? No lies, no lawsuits, no feuds?

"No, nothing at all."

His only mistake? Naming the place after himself. In Scotland, "Trump Turnberry" goes over like "Trump Versailles" would in France or "Trump Rushmore" in America. The name pisses Scots off. "I refuse to say it that way," says Huggan. "I refuse to put those two words together in my mouth and nobody can make me say it that way."

When Trump changed the famous lighthouse logo to his own crest and slapped a big "Trump Turnberry" above it, the pro shop merchandise sold like anthrax cupcakes. Finally, somebody convinced Trump to get rid of his logo and go back to the old one without his name. That worked. You go in the pro shop now and you can hardly find a stitch of Trump stuff. "It all hit the clearance sale table," one Turnberry employee told me. "I got a 200-quid bag for 40!"

That's just one reason Trump is bleeding money at Turnberry. According to Bloomberg, Trump Turnberry lost $36 million in 2016 against revenues of only $12 million. That debt load doubled from the previous year.

It's too bad. Turnberry is so much better under Trump. Take the lighthouse. It used to just sit there by the 9th tee, looking a lot like Melania, gorgeous and lonely. There's even a splendid halfway house at the base of it now and two luxurious guest suites in the top half. I was sitting on the porch of it on the day Trump was to arrive from his chaotic meeting with British prime minister Theresa May in July of 2018. Word was, Eric Trump was ensconced in the suite for the weekend. There were snipers in the turret above. I saw somebody I recognized: Keith Thomas, one of the president's military aides who carries the "nuclear football," the satchel that contains the codes for the president to launch a nuclear attack. He didn't have the satchel with him, though, he had a lemonade. He was admiring the Firth of Clyde and, in the distance, Northern Ireland.

"Sorry about the view," I said.

He jumped up and practically saluted. "Yes, sir, it is! Never been here before."

I asked him if his boss would be arriving by Marine One.

"No, sir," he said. "We're trying to be low key in Scotland, so he's coming in by motorcade."

Well, "low key" is in the eye of the beholder. Trump would be landing in Air Force One at nearby Prestwick Airport, along with a C-17, which carries The Beast presidential limo and other security vehicles, and a third plane full of press and officials, plus a military fighter jet escort or two, plus God knows what else. When they arrived, they'd also find Eric Trump's helicopter parked garishly on the hotel lawn, with giant letters spelling "TRUMP" on the side.

I couldn't resist asking Thomas about "the green box," the Port-O-Let-sized container that's always with the president—a bombproof, bulletproof tiny fortress they can shove him into if things get hairy. "Does it have food and water inside?" I asked.

He laughed. "Hmmmm. I don't know, sir. I'll have to find that out for you."

Yes, get back to me first thing in the morning.

I asked him how he thought the planned anti-Trump protests would go the next morning. There'd already been some that morning on the road in front ("You're Not Welcome Here"), and there were more planned all over the nation, including giant ones in Edinburgh, Glasgow, and, of course, Aberdeen and Balmedie.

"I think it will be fine," Thomas said. "These Scottish people are so nice. Even the protesters are nice. It's kind of hard to hate them."

He's right. Protests in Scotland are just a notch below a picnic. For a solid week in 2016, there was a comedian named Janey Godley who would stand on the road that runs in front of the Turnberry hotel holding up a sign that read: "Trump Is a Cunt." Each day, the hotel staff would invite her in for lunch and tea. One time, on a freezing, rainy winter day, a man kept marching back and forth on the street, holding up his anti-Trump sign. The guys in the bag room insisted he come inside, warm up, and eat a cheeseburger.

That early evening, the motorcade arrived. There was heavy security everywhere. Trump was having his picture taken on the grand front steps of the hotel with patrons and family when—stunningly—a Greenpeace protester flying a microlight flew right over him, not even 30 feet above, making three loops. How he got past all the military and Secret Service and security aircraft, who knows. He was flying a flag behind him that read: "Trump—Well Below Par."

"I couldn't believe it," said Tim Size, an American from St. Louis who was standing right there. "It was right above us. I thought sure the snipers would shoot him down. He could've had a bomb or a gun—anything. But they didn't. He just flew away. We asked one of the Secret Service guys later why they didn't shoot. He said, 'If we'd been back home, we would've. But not in Scotland.' "

After a long pause, Secret Service rushed Trump inside the hotel. Once inside, according to two sources who were there, Trump later asked his wife, "What'd the banner say?"

" 'Well below par'," Melania answered.

"Beautiful!" Trump exulted. "I WANT to be below par!"

Greenpeace protesters do not play a lot of golf.

The next morning, as Thomas predicted, the protesters were everywhere, in the sheep fields and on the roads leading in and out, as they were all over the Scottish nation, with a rage they hadn't shown to an American president since Nixon, if that. They even wrote messages in the sand at Balmedie in hopes Trump would fly over ("Putin's Pussy"). He never did.

Trump saw them as he began his golf round. They chanted and yelled at him: "Racist!" "Cunt!" and "Fuckhead!" And what did he do? He waved at them as though they were fans. Gave them the big hi hello.

Admit it. The guy is clever.

As usual, Trump was playing that day in a cart. Trump always plays in a cart. The only problem with that is that, at both Aberdeen and Turnberry, you must have a signed doctor's letter to take a cart. They want you to walk. Yet there he was.

Despite all the people, protesters, and press around, Trump still cheated.

"I'm shooting him on the second fairway," says Scottish photographer Stuart Wallace. "And I see a Secret Service agent kick his ball out of the rough. The [agent] was in a buggy up ahead of him and [Trump's] drive ended up in the rough and he got out of his buggy and kicked it out on the short stuff. Unbelievable."

Afterward, a Turnberry caddy emailed me. He'd never seen Trump play before. "He had 4 or 5 hacks out of one bunker before hand-wedging it onto the green!"

The next day, after the Trump circus left town, a very pro-Trump Texan came to Turnberry. He took at a look at the obligatory massive flag flapping from the trademark 100-foot pole by the first tee and wrinkled his nose. He was expecting the stars and stripes and wasn't seeing it, only the white and blue of the Scottish flag.

"Hey," the Texan asked a caddy, "Is that a new Trump flag or somethin'?"

Give him time.

7

TACKY IS AS TACKY DOES

I only do 10s.
—DONALD J. TRUMP

TRUMP IS NOT JUST a political outlier. He's a golf outlier. Forget how he plays the game. Just in the simplest politeness of the game, the timeless etiquette of it, Trump seems to have come from another planet.

For instance, he never takes off his hat for the traditional end-of-round handshake, which is considered gentlemanly. He doesn't take it off inside the clubhouse, either, which is a little golf-gauche. He doesn't care whose honor it is on the tee box, either. He just steps up first and hits it. He's not what you'd call a good loser, either.

"I played with him once," says *Los Angeles Times* NFL writer Sam Farmer. "And I actually beat him out of $10. He handed me the two fives, but they wouldn't quite come out of his hand. He held onto them and made me pull. I thought they were going to rip. When I finally got them, he goes, 'It's all right. I've got a supermodel girlfriend and my own 727, so I'm okay.' "

There's a famous story about the time Trump lost $50 to a guy at Winged Foot. Trump said he didn't have any cash. "That's okay," the guy said. "I'll take a check."

Trump said he didn't have any checks on him.

"That's okay, I'll take a bank draft. I'll go get it." So the guy gets in his car and gets a bank draft for $50, brings it back, and Trump signs it. Weeks later, Trump sees him, pissed off.

"You cashed my check!"

"Of course I did."

"Nobody *ever* cashes my checks. They frame them!"

This is a man who famously drives his golf cart on greens. To repeat: He drives ON THE GREEN. There is video of him doing it at Trump Bedminster. In golf, that's the unholiest-of-unholies. Driving your cart on the green is like hanging your laundry in the Sistine Chapel. A green is a tender and delicate thing. Caddies don't even set their bags on it. Driving on the green leaves tire tracks on the perfect surface that can send your partner's putt careening off line, not to mention the putts of the 100 players behind you. I've met people who were 100% for Trump politically but vow they'll never vote for him again because he drove on the green. Says one woman, "That's such a violation!"

"He did it all the time at Doral," says Joe Santilli, a former member there. "He'd come along with five or six people and play through us, never asking permission, just playing through. And he'd drive his cart right on the green."

I hear you: *It's his course. He gets to do what he wants.* But there's a line, and driving a cart on a green is about three national parks past it. If you go to a friend's house for dinner, does that mean he has the right to come out of his bedroom drunk in his half-open bathrobe and plunk himself down on your wife's lap?

"He drives across tees, too," says a source inside Bedminster. "The guy walks as little as possible. He gets out, walks two feet, hits, and gets back in the cart."

Very hard to get your 10,000 steps that way.

Chefs don't call Michelin asking for an extra star. Actors don't go on TV saying they deserve an Oscar. And golf course developers don't beg to be on Top 100 golf course lists.

Except Trump. He begs, bullies, and badgers the magazines that do the ratings. When he's not happy with the ratings he gets, he'll rip them out of the magazine, scrawl something nasty on them with a Sharpie—"DISHONEST!"—and mail them to the editor.

Since he unveiled his first course in 1999, Trump International in West Palm Beach, Trump has wheedled, lobbied, and lied ceaselessly hyping them. The higher the rankings, the more he can charge for memberships and guest fees. Rankings, though, are a number he can't Trump Bump and it drives him crazy.

For instance, he's said repeatedly that Trump Los Angeles is better than Pebble Beach. Now, understand, Pebble Beach is universally thought of as one of the most beautiful courses in the world. It's been ranked the best course in the world hundreds of times. It's held five U.S. Opens, which have been won by no less than Jack Nicklaus, Tom Watson, and Tiger Woods. For many touring pros, it's the place they'd play if they only had one round left. So to say Trump Los Angeles is better than Pebble Beach is a family-sized jar of stupid sauce.

Yes, Trump Los Angeles has stunning views of the Pacific, but that's all it's got. "It's a plate of sausages," says architect Robert Trent Jones, Jr. In golf-design lingo, a "plate of sausages" means it's laid out like somebody laying sausages all in the same direction, packed onto the platter. I've played it. Once was enough. Seventeen holes run parallel to the ocean, back and forth, over and over again, until you feel like you're on a boot camp march. Only one hole, the first, goes perpendicular. Says golf architect Tom Doak, "Nobody in the world thinks his course is better than Pebble—except Donald Trump."

It gets so ridiculous at Trump Los Angeles that, no joke, they don't even like to see the Pebble Beach logo. "I walked in there once wearing a Pebble Beach shirt," says L.A. golf marketer Robert Ward. "The general manager says, 'Is there any way you can change your shirt? Mr. Trump really doesn't like to see that logo.' I'm not kidding. And Trump wasn't even around."

Trump was never on the Wharton debating team, but he employs some masterful rhetorical tricks when flogging his courses. For instance, when Trump lies, he doubles down by making his enemies complicit in his side of the argument. Take, for instance, what he says about his Trump Philadelphia course in Pine Hill, New Jersey, which has the misfortune to be a 10-minute drive from the universally acknowledged and current No. 1 course in the world—Pine Valley (NJ). Being next door to Pine Valley is sort of like being Penelope Cruz's foster sister. Still, Trump has said, repeatedly, "It is as good as Pine Valley, if not better....I really believe it. A lot of the people there are saying so. And if you went there, you would say it, too. Everybody that goes there says it."

(Let's pause here for the world's golfers to slap their foreheads in unison.)

I went to Trump Philadelphia and...no, no, a million times no. It's not in the same galaxy as Pine Valley. Since *Golf Digest* began ranking courses, no other property has finished No. 1 in America as many times as Pine Valley. Trump Philadelphia, meanwhile, has never made their top 200. It isn't even ranked in the top 15 courses in the state of New Jersey.

"It's the same soil!" Trump insists.

BUYER: Why are you charging Park Ave prices for this Hell's Kitchen tenement building?
TRUMP: Same soil!

Even his buddy Tom Fazio giggles at this one. "He tells reporters, 'People are telling me this is better than Pine Valley.' But he never says who those people are. Do you know who the people are? They're the people who work for him, like his caddies. He will be like, 'Hey Mario, don't you think this is better than Pine Valley?' And Mario will go, 'Oh yeah! Much better!'...I honestly think he believes the things he says. He hears himself say it and pretty soon he completely believes it."

Put it this way, Trump keeps a locker there, but, according to the members and employees I spoke to, hadn't been there since 2015. If it were better than the No. 1 ranked course in the world, you think he might swing by now and again?

It drives Trump out of his brain when other courses are ranked above his or when his courses don't make the lists at all. He lies and tells people the reason his courses go unranked is because, "I don't let the raters on my courses. I don't want to bother the membership." But that's a fat lie. The truth is, he's dying to get on the lists. It's a game he can't control and can't fudge and can't buy, so it vexes his sleep.

One night, in March of 2014, an editor and writer at *Golfweek* named Jeff Babineau answered his home phone. It was Larry Glick, Trump's right-hand golf man, saying Trump would be calling in five minutes. "Take the call," Glick instructed.

Trump called. He was hot. *Golfweek* has two lists: Top 100 Classic (pre-1960) and Top 100 Modern (post-1960). Trump's new Doral makeover had finished just after the deadline for *Golfweek's* 700 to 800 raters to see it. But Trump begged *Golfweek* to extend the deadline and they gave in. A group of raters were rushed through as a favor for one of the biggest golf developers in the country. So the raters hurried over, heard Trump say, "Doral is the greatest course in Florida!," played it, huddled together, and ranked it No. 99 on the Modern list. Now, for perspective, there are 15,000-plus golf courses in the United States, and to be recognized in the top 100 is really good. But good is not nearly good enough for Donald Trump. He heard about the 99 and was fried about it.

Rrrrring, rrrrring.

"Hello?" Babineau said.

"You need to take Doral out of your rankings," Trump barked, skipping the customary opening greetings. "Take it out now."

"Is this Mr. Trump?"

"Yes. Take it out."

"Well, first of all," Babineau tried to explain, "the rankings are already in print. They'll be in the next magazine."

"Doral needs to come out," Trump insisted. "Take the course out."

Babineau said he couldn't do that and wouldn't do that. Trump then began to harp on the *Golfweek* writer in charge of the ratings, Bradley Klein.

"Klein's an idiot," Trump kept saying. "You have an idiot in charge of your rankings."

Trump insisted this was more order than request. Doral had to come out of their rankings because...just because. He was hinting at removing all his advertising from *Golfweek*, and...who knows what?

Babineau sighed and finally said, "Then I suppose you want ALL of the Trump properties out of the rankings, right?"

"Such as?"

"Well, for one, Trump International Scotland is in our Great Britain and Ireland Modern rankings."

"Where do you have that ranked?"

"No. 1."

Pause.

"Well, at least you got SOMETHING right."

Doral stayed in at 99.

The long-suffering Klein is used to this from Trump. "He [Trump] started calling me about eight or nine years ago," Klein says. "I was driving in Phoenix, and Donald calls me, and all of a sudden he starts yelling at me because Trump National [Bedminster] Old Course [wasn't] high enough. 'It's the greatest course,' 'It's better than this, better than that,' on and on and on. He's ranting and raving. At one point, he says, 'I don't know what I have to do. I'll do anything you want me to do. I'll call up the publisher and if you want me to, I'll buy ads.'"

Klein finally had to get him off the line. He said, "Mr. Trump, I can't have this conversation. You're fired."

When Trump can't get what he wants from editors, he starts hammering the salespeople. "He'd say, 'If I'm not No. 1, then I don't want to be in at all,'" says one golf magazine salesperson who asked not to be identified. "Then he'd call and say the Trump properties were too exclusive to be ranked. Don't rank them. He called me once and said, 'You make my course No. 1, and you don't have to work anymore.' To which I answered, 'Well, I'm going to have to work tomorrow. That's just not possible.'"

If you simply agree that Trump courses should all be ranked

No. 1, you'll get along really well with him. Once, in discussing Trump Washington, he told *Golf Digest's* David Owen that it "blows away Congressional [a famous D.C. club that has hosted two U.S. Opens] like nobody ever blew it away. They say it's not even a contest."

Congressional is ranked 80th by *Golf Digest* among U.S. courses. Trump Washington is good but unranked. It's not in their Top 200 list either. It doesn't even make their Best 10 Courses in Virginia. So he's right. It's not even a contest.

Trump once tweeted that he was about to go play Trump International (West Palm Beach), "the number-one rated golf course in the State of Florida."

Okay…no. I've never seen a reputable ranking of Trump International as the best in Florida. It's not within a par 5 of the best course in Florida, a state with so many great golf courses it should count as its own country. Seminole, for instance, is a gem and unrivaled in the state. It's ranked 12 in America. The unforgettable TPC Sawgrass (Stadium) and its first-ever island green is ranked 49. I could go on. "I can probably name 25 courses in South Florida alone that are better," says longtime PGA Tour star Mark Calcavecchia. "I mean, there's nothing wrong with [Trump International], but it's nothing amazing." It's ranked 156th by *Golf Digest*.

To be sure, Trump has some fine courses. Trump Bedminster is very good. It's already held a U.S. Women's Open and will hold the 2022 PGA Championship, a major. Trump's course in Aberdeen, Scotland, is sensational to look at, albeit a bastardization of a links course. His Turnberry is so much better under Trump that it's crazy it's currently not scheduled to hold another Open Championship.

The problem is, Trump insists they're ALL wonderful. "Every one of my courses is, like, amazing," Trump said once. Really? Because if you're speaking of your Trump National Hudson Valley, it isn't even America's best golf course named Hudson. (Hudson National is 81st.) If you're talking about Trump Colts Neck, that's just a muni with a fancy clubhouse and high dues. If you're talking about Doonbeg in Ireland, you must be, as the Irish say, "thick as a plank."

Course raters for magazines are not allowed to give interviews, but I got a major American golf magazine rater to explain why Trump's American courses don't break an egg with them.

"They're mostly big boring Fazios," the rater says. "Whether it's Tom or Jim or the nephew (Tommy). But that's what Trump wants. He's a maximalist. The bigger, the better, the waterfalls. The other problem is the land they sit on isn't interesting. So when really new, interesting courses come along, like Bandon Dunes or Friar's Head, they're going to push the big, boring courses off the list. I mean, you look at his courses and there's not one that deserves it. Doral is only for the big Tour bombers now. Trump Jupiter is his best course in Florida, but it's not good enough. Trump Philadelphia is crap—way too steep. His courses in Charlotte, Washington, Hudson Valley, Colts Neck—those are all big yawners. Trump invited as many raters as he could get to Trump L.A. and that backfired because that course is a real piece of sh*t. Trump Ferry Point, though, is really good for a public course (95th on *Golf Digest*'s Top 100 Public Courses), but otherwise, no. No way."

There are a lot of lists, though, and as we've seen, sometimes a Trump course will find its way on one. The first time Bedminster made a list, there happened to be a press event there and his then-chairman of Bedminster, Ashley Cooper, stood up with a secret that he just couldn't contain any longer. With great pride, dressed in a beautiful summer suit, Cooper revealed that Bedminster would be showing up at No. 47 in the upcoming top American course rankings for *Golf* magazine. Cooper was practically bursting with pride.

Then Trump stepped up. "I know Ashley's happy we're 47th," Trump grumbled, "but I think 47th sucks."

Once, Trump was asked to make his own ranking. Which were the top 10 courses in the country, did he think? It read:

1. Trump Bedminster
2. Winged Foot
3. Trump Westchester
4. Trump West Palm Beach
5. Augusta National
6. Cypress Point
7. Trump Los Angeles
8. Oakmont
9. Trump Philadelphia
10. Pebble Beach

What? No Trump Ferry Point?

Trump's rankings-grubbing strategy has two prongs: (1) Lie about the greatness of his courses and (2) Rip everybody else's.

To wit:

Bandon Dunes in Oregon is America's purest golf destination. Set in the wilderness against breathtaking cliffs, waves, and sand dunes, it's all caddies and no carts, flabbergasting beauty, steak and whiskey and cigars around the outdoor fireplaces afterward. It might even have America's best par-3 course, a 13-hole jewel designed by Ben Crenshaw and Bill Coore, plus it has the Punchbowl, a rolling, football-sized putting course with waitresses in long gowns serving you cocktails as you gamble, laugh, and savor another perfect sunset.

Trump despises Bandon Dunes, saying it's set in a "vast wasteland." Up against his Aberdeen and Turnberry courses, he called it "a toy by comparison." Some toy. All four of Bandon Dunes courses were ranked in *Golf Digest*'s 2019–2020 America's Top 100 Courses: Pacific Dunes is 17, Bandon Dunes 36, Old McDonald 50, and Bandon Trails 69. There are zero Trump courses on the latest list.

But here's the funny thing: By all accounts, Trump has never *been* to Bandon Dunes. "I checked with a bunch of my guys up there," says architect Doak, "and not one of them had ever heard of him coming." I did the same. I go to Bandon once a year, and nobody I know who works there had ever seen Trump, either. "We have no record of him ever being here," says Michael Chupka, Bandon's director of communications.

Doak took it a step further. "I called a friend of mine who knows [Trump] and said, 'Hey, next time you see Trump, ask him if he's been to Bandon Dunes?'" The friend called back and reported, "Donald said, 'No,' but some of his friends have and 'they say it's nowhere near as good as Aberdeen.' So that tells you everything you need to know."

Trump doesn't do golf trips with buddies, and he rarely builds golf courses outside of the northeast or Florida or L.A. He's only got one American course outside of those areas—Charlotte—and anybody who lives in Charlotte will tell you he almost never goes there. You could tell that when he got up at a rally in Charlotte in the summer of 2018 and said that his golf course sat along the "largest manmade lake in the world, by far." Wrong, by far. His course sits along Lake Norman, which is not only *not* the world's largest man-made lake, it's not even among the top 10 biggest reservoirs in the U.S.

Trump likes golf courses the way he builds them and everybody else can turn theirs into parking lots. He likes lush green grass, big water features—"the more water, the better for Donald," Fazio says—and Pentagon-sized clubhouses anchored by 80-foot flagpoles. Nothing else will do.

Exhibit A: When they played the 2014 U.S. Open at the classic Pinehurst (NC) No. 2, Trump excoriated it in a tweetstorm:

I have numerous courses that are far superior to Pinehurst.

I'd bet the horrible look of Pinehurst translates into poor television ratings. This is not what golf is about!

To which longtime *USA Today* golf writer Steve DiMeglio added, wryly:

Maybe needs 1 of your waterfalls.

But here's the thing: Trump wasn't AT the U.S. Open. He was watching it on TV. He complained that the greens "looked terrible" on TV and it was a disservice to the game to have the Open on such a dump. But if you were there, you knew how sensational the setup was. The best greens do not necessarily look great on TV. The best greens are a patchwork of different grasses, a combination that produces the purest surface that rewards the truest putters. Sometimes that gives a green that looks a little brown on TV. It's the kind of linksy land golf was invented on, watered by the rain, mowed by hungry sheep, natural and true. But Trump hates it. What can brown do for Trump? Nothing.

Exhibit B: His waterfalls.

"Jesus, the waterfalls," says architect Jones. "I like waterfalls if they're natural. But the kind of phony waterfall he builds, I hate. It's artificial. It's in your face. It's Las Vegas. It's clownish. But it IS in keeping with his character."

As you stand next to Trump's 101-foot waterfall at Westchester, trying to putt, you find out it's very, very loud.

YOU: I think you're away.
FRIEND: What???
YOU: I THINK YOU'RE AWAY!!!
FRIEND: YES, IT IS A NICE DAY!

When Trump Los Angeles opened, it had a giant fake waterfall behind the first hole, thundering so loudly you wondered if a tsunami was coming. Worse, when you were done with the hole, the cart path brought you within inches of it, getting the passenger wet, as though you were playing Trump Splash Mountain. Yeah, you're wet, but you only have 17 more holes to go.

Trump insisted on a waterfall at West Palm Beach, too. He also has one at Trump Washington, an otherwise wonderful course, wandering as it does along the Potomac and among the ponds and bogs near it. It's just you, the eagles, and the wind on a really good golf course. Until, that is, you make the turn back to the clubhouse at 18, when, out of nowhere, a giant mountainous waterfall rears up behind the green. This thing is the Iguazu of Trump waterfalls. It pumps 25 gallons a minute and is so huge and fake that on the flattened top of it there's room for 200 guests to fit comfortably for weddings, of which there are dozens and dozens, members say.

"He's got a thing for the waterfalls," chuckles Fazio, who designed Trump Washington, D.C., with lots of input from Trump. "I remember he and I were on the site one day. There's a ravine behind the 18th green. And Donald hollers at [his contractor], 'Frank! Frank! I need a big waterfall here!'" Later, some of my people said, 'Tom you can't let him do this! It's going to look ridiculous!' And I told them, 'Are you nuts? He's the boss. As long as I get paid, I don't care.'"

Trump's taste is Early Whatever Reminds You He's Rich. When he gave me a tour of his Trump Tower apartment in New York City, the views were incredible, 270 degrees. But it all looked a little like Liberace's bathroom. Everything was dripping in gold, crystal, or white gold–trimmed crystal. I sat down at a beautiful white grand piano and asked if I could play. It was hopelessly out of tune. Clearly, nobody had played it in years. "Oh, man, he was SO pissed you said his piano was out of tune," reports *Sports Illustrated* writer Michael Bamberger, who has played golf nine times with Trump. "He was like, 'That sonofabitch Reilly said my piano was out of tune! That piano is NOT out of tune!'" He's probably right. I only play piano an hour a day. What would I know?

There was a huge, gold telescope in the corner of the apartment, pointing downtown. I looked through it and was amazed at its power.

"I watched the Twin Towers come down through that," Trump said over my shoulder.

I pulled my head away from the telescope and looked at him in shock. "Oh, my god," I said.

Trump nodded with pride and said, "Solid gold."

Greeting arrivals at nearly every Trump course is an Italian marble–belching over-the-top fountain, featuring four Poseidons, seven growling lions, and gallons of spouting water. It looks like it should be on Mike Tyson's lawn. "When he first put that in, we were all like, 'Oh, my god, how gaudy can you get?'" says Trump Washington member Gary Newman. "But now we don't even see it."

One thing you can't help seeing at Trump Washington is a Civil War memorial near the 14th hole, which overlooks the Potomac River. It reads:

The River of Blood

Many great American soldiers, both of the North and South, died at this spot, "The Rapids," on the Potomac River. The casualties were so great that the water would turn red and thus became known as "The River of Blood." It is my great honor to have preserved this important section of the Potomac River!

—Donald John Trump

It's a very nice monument except for one little problem: It didn't happen. No battle like that occurred anywhere near the monument. Three different Civil War historians confirmed the lie. That's when the fun started.

"How would they know that?" Trump replied when confronted by the *New York Times*. "Were they there?"

He's right, of course. Were you at Gettysburg? Then how do you know what Lincoln said? When the *Times* trotted out the names of its three prominent Civil War historians, Trump trotted out his own vague army of them. "I was told that by numerous historians," Trump said.

Fine. Names please?

Uh, well, he couldn't remember their names. Besides, he said, he hadn't talked to the historians himself. His team had.

Fine. Give us your staff names and we'll get their sources.

Trump refused. "Write your story the way you want to," he said. "But many people were shot there. It makes sense."

No, it's bullshit. I checked with Loudon County spokesman Glen Barbour, who looked into it and emailed that "the county was not aware of any historical significance on the property." That was just immoral. What Trump did next was illegal. He cut down 450 trees along the Potomac River, the better for his members to see it. That's illegal in Loudon County without permission, and nobody gave it to him, according to Barbour. He says the county was on a simple inspection there in 2010 when they discovered the tree-asco. They issued a stop-work order on any more changes, not to be lifted until Trump paid a hefty fine for cutting down all those trees, and restabilized the river bank. Bottom line? Trump got what he wanted without waiting and let his people sweep up the mess, as usual.

That little trick caused even more upheaval, though. By removing the trees, the Secret Service decided it gave snipers a clear shot. So they decided nobody could boat or canoe on the river while the president was on the course, which angered fisherman, companies that transport goods on the river, and local canoeists, who sued.

But the fibbing doesn't end there. Keep looking at that Civil War memorial for a second. Below you can see the Trump family coat of arms, which sports three lions and two chevrons on a shield below a gloved hand gripping an arrow. The motto reads, "Numquam Concedere"—latin for "Never Concede," truly Trump's philosophy.

It's a beautiful coat of arms, except for one small problem: Trump stole it.

It's actually the 80-year-old family crest granted by British authorities in 1939 to Joseph Edward Davies, the third husband of Marjorie Merriweather Post, the socialite who built Mar-a-Lago, now Trump's combo Winter White House/social and golf club. Trump made only one small adjustment to it—replacing the word "integritas" (Latin for "integrity") with "Trump." (Yes, he took out "integrity" and replaced it with "Trump." Some of this stuff writes itself.)

Mr. Davies was ambassador to Belgium and served as a special envoy for President Truman. Trump liked the Davies family crest and began passing it off as his own. He now uses it everywhere, on Trump golf towels, on Trump golf balls, even on the toilet paper in the luxurious men's room stalls at his clubs. Yes, the toilet paper has his name on it. Not sure he thought that one all the way through.

Trump never asked permission to take the Davies family coat of arms. If he had, he'd have had to call Davies' grandson, lawyer Joseph D. Tydings, a Democrat and former U.S. senator from Maryland. And what would Tydings have said? Take it. "You don't sue Trump," Tydings explains, "because you'll be in court for years and years and years." He talked his family out of suing Trump over the whole mess years ago. He told them it would be an endless and costly exercise. Still, he admits, his grandfather "would be rolling over in his grave to think Trump was using his crest."

Free to fly the fake family flag, Trump figured, "Why not take it to Scotland?" So he did. It turns out the Scots don't take family crests so lightly. It's a criminal offense to steal another family's coat of arms. Scots do not bullshit around about family crests. Scotland heritage authorities ordered Trump to cease and desist or face criminal charges. Trump sued, naturally, in 2007. Five years later, he lost and finally gave up, motto or no motto. He changed enough things on the crest to get around the law, including replacing the lions with a two-headed eagle (repre-senting his Scottish and German roots) clutching golf balls. The two-headed eagle also happens to be the official crest of Russia.

Of course, Trump's European heritage isn't all that regal. His grandfather once owned a hotel in Canada that dabbled in prostitution.

Now *that* would be a family crest.

8

YOUR DAY IN TRUMPLAND

He who has the fastest golf cart never has a bad lie.
—MICKEY MANTLE

REALLY? YOU HAVE A tee time with the President of the Freaking United States?

Okay, brace yourself, because what you're about to experience isn't really golf. It's more of a para-military heavily armed exercise with odd-shaped sticks, using a vague set of rules that requires you to lose, and it will all be over very quickly so put your memory on "save."

First of all, you'll play at one of Trump's courses—since he's been president, he's played *only* at his own courses. He hasn't played once anywhere else, even at the only un-Trump course where he's a member: Winged Foot Golf Club in Mamaroneck, New York.

Me, I'd rent a car. Yours could get egged by protesters. With Trump spending so much time at his courses, thousands of Trump resisters have come to realize it's a great place to remind him how much they loathe him. As a result, the police blotters in Trump golf towns make fabulous Cheerios reading. For instance:

- A woman wrote a Spanish slur in lipstick on the entrance sign to Trump Los Angeles. The man she was with peed on it.
- About 200 activists laid down on the front lawn of Trump Los Angeles and formed a human-body message reading: "RESIST!"
- A woman took a cornfield near Trump Bedminster and carved into it the words "VOTE" and "TRUTH" in letters 60 feet high and 75 feet wide.
- Video posted by the *Washington Post* appeared to show at least four individuals in dark clothing using gardening tools to carve six-foot-tall letters into the green at Trump Los Angeles spelling out: "NO MORE TIGERS, NO MORE WOODS."
- A 61-year-old man named Cliff Tillotson, owner of a successful construction firm in Hawaii, was charged with turning Trump golf greens into a kind of giant message board. At four different Trump courses, Tillotson allegedly used a chemical to write into dozens of greens things like, "If Jesus came back tomorrow he wouldn't be an evangelical," "Product of too much Propecia" (a slap at Trump's use of a hair-loss drug), and an entire soliloquy from *Macbeth*. Personally, I've never had a putt over an entire Shakespearian soliloquy, but it has to be a *bitch* to read.

Every Saturday, the "People's Motorcade," as they call them-selves, drives up and down outside the Bedminster gates carry-ing on with all kinds of anti-Trump signs and hijinks. There's the truck with an effigy of Trump in the back complete with a Pinocchio nose. Oh, and for the trips when Trump choppers in, they've laid out a giant "FU45" near the landing pad for his viewing pleasure.

Because Trump once planned to build a family mausoleum on his Bedminster property (he now wants to be buried at Mar-a-Lago), protesters are dying all over the place. One day, at a major intersection near the front gates, about 30 people held a "die in," laying on the ground, holding tombstones labeled with pre-existing conditions. A group called INDECLINE built an elaborate and extraordinary "Trump Cemetery" with realis-tic tombstones marking the deaths of "Decency," "The American Dream," and "The Last Snowman."

Anyway, I hope you get to play Trump Bedminster, in New Jersey, because there's nothing quite like it. Just to become a member can cost you up to $300,000. It was once the country estate of car tycoon John DeLorean, who would let his friend Jackie O ride her horse there among the pastoral hither and yon. It's 45 minutes from Manhattan and 10 exits past the fanciest place you've ever been. Its two courses are pretty good, the ser-vice is immaculate, and the interiors are just slightly more lavish than a sultan's dream. Enjoy the one-mile tree-lined driveway that takes you to a place that's a cross between Augusta National and the Paris Ritz, only with sniper towers.

It's literally true. When the 2017 U.S. Women's Open finished at Trump Bedminster that summer, Fox started dismantling its camera towers. *Hold on,* the Secret Service said. *We'd like to buy that tower.* Now, whenever Trump is at Bedminster, there are two snipers in that tower, one looking out toward the course, the other watching over the swanky compound that includes Trump's cottage (read: mansion), Ivanka's cottage (ditto), and eight other actual rental cottages (luxurious), all surrounding a fabulous pool, lounge, and, one imagines, people in togas peeling grapes for you.

Bedminster might be Trump's favorite place in the world. It has 36 holes, and unlike Mar-a-Lago, he doesn't have to drag the 10 SUVs, the Beast presidential limo, and the SWAT team over to Trump International to play. It's all right outside his front door. Ivanka and husband Jared Kushner spend lots of weekends at their cottage for the same reason. On Shabbat, they can simply walk the 100 yards to dinner without driving. Trump Bedminster is one of three official residences of the president—along with Trump Tower and Mar-a-Lago—which means Congress allotted $41 million in 2017 to its official protection. His 17-day vacation there in August of 2018 cost taxpayers over $3 million.

"Gotta be 300 Secret Service, Marines, SWAT, everything," the Bedminster car valet told me. "You know he's coming because you hear the choppers. There's always three—Marine One, Marine Two, and a Blackhawk—so nobody knows which one he's in. They land right over there." He pointed to a helicopter pad near the compound.

Q: Why doesn't Trump ever go to the legendary Camp David

in Maryland, traditionally the summer getaway spot for presidents and a place pre-set for security?

A: Because Camp David is for suckers. "Camp David is very rustic, it's nice, you'd like it," Trump said in an interview with a European journalist in 2017. "You know how long you'd like it? For about 30 minutes."

Okay, you're here. You'll be directed to the locker room to change shoes. With golf carts, almost nobody sweats anymore playing golf, so golf locker rooms are pointless except as a way to feel rich, and Trump very much wants you to feel rich. Trump locker rooms are spectacular. When you walk, the marble squeaks under your feet. Drink the Trump coffee (out of business) or the Trump vodka (out of business) or the Trump water (out of business). Sink deeply into the leather couches and eat some Trump nuts (out of business). Go find his locker. At every American Trump course I visited, he had one, sometimes full size, sometimes half, always locked. Sometimes, the clubhouse guys get so sick of guests taking selfies in front of it, they tape over the nameplate.

Now it's time to go hit a few warm-up shots on the practice range. This is where you'll see Trump for the first time. He'll greet you like a nephew greets his Lotto-winning uncle. He'll give you the big 20-second, pull-you-in handshake. The left hand will be on your right shoulder. He'll make you feel like a visiting king.

Trump is not big on practice. He'll whack a few and want to go to the first tee. If you're playing the Old Course at Bedminster, check out the cool plaque there. It reads:

This is the best design I've ever done.
—Tom Fazio

Turns out the plaque misquoted him. "I don't believe I said it exactly like that," Fazio texted me. "It's kinda like him calling you the publisher of *Sports Illustrated*. Sounds better."

Bring your A game because you'll be playing with decent golfers. Trump doesn't suffer hacks. They take too long. If there's a politician in the group, he will almost certainly be a Republican. Through 2018, Trump hadn't played with a single Democratic member of Congress or state governor, despite reaming out Obama in a 2012 tweet for the same thing:

Obama should play golf with Republicans & opponents rather than his small group of friends. That way maybe the terrible gridlock would end.

You will not believe the security around you. There can be as many as 60 Secret Service agents, six SWAT guys, and 30 carts following along as you play, holding, among other things:

- The nuclear football
- The assistant chief of staff
- A doctor with vials of Trump's blood
- A communications staff member
- The secure satellite phone
- The one-man portable bomb shelter

- An entire supply of gas masks, machine guns, and weapons
- A small missile, which really speeds up play

"I couldn't believe what has to happen to get him around the course," says 1989 Open Championship winner Mark Calcavecchia, who was teeing off one day at Trump International in Florida around the same time as Trump. "Just in front of the club, there was a fire truck, an ambulance, 10 black SUVs, police cars, dogs, everything. On the course, there were at least two Secret Service guys and at least one cart on every hole.

"Anyway, we finally teed off and he was about two or three groups behind us. We've got four holes left and now here he is, coming through us. They basically strip-searched us in the middle of the fairway. We all got patted down in case we had a gun out there. Anyway, we go into the dining room after. He was in there eating. I had to go through two or three detectors just to get to the dining room. I'm like, 'Hey, man, we were just searched on the course. What do you think happened in five holes?'"

The story goes that one day when Trump was playing Bedminster, a member hit an unspeakable hook not just deep into the woods but bound for I-78. As the caddy was looking for it, he suddenly found four machine gun barrels in his face, all held by camouflaged Marines. So, the perimeter is covered, in case you were wondering.

Yes, other groups can still play when the president is playing, as long as they're willing to stand down when he comes through, and he will come through. Trump plays breathtakingly fast—"When you pick up every putt within six feet, you can do that," says one caddy—and it means the vanguard of the Secret Service has to work faster. You'll be playing along at Bedminster when two Secret Service golf carts will come up quickly and stop you mid-6 iron.

"Gentlemen," the agent will say. "Will you please step to the side of the fairway? The president is coming through."

PLAYER: Sure. What hole is he on?

AGENT: 8.

PLAYER: But we're on 11.

AGENT, LOUDER: Yes. Will you please stand aside?

You won't have to wait long. Soon enough, Trump will come barreling through, charming and friendly, shaking everybody's hand, thanking them for waiting, asking them how their round is going. He'll even take pictures with you. "Just don't post it on social media," he'll say, and they've almost all complied.

Okay, time to quiet the knocking of your knees and hit that first shot. Not to worry, Trump will make it fun. Playing with Trump, everybody has fun. He'll pay attention to you. He'll ask a thousand questions. *How's business? How much you pay for that putter? You wanna sell it?* He'll give you tips and he'll know what he's talking about. *You gotta come more from underneath, like this!* You'll be answering his questions and working on his lesson and trying to keep up, and it will all be a big bowl of crazy.

Bill Clinton once said, "I love playing with him. He outdrives me on every single hole, but I forgive him."

Don't expect a lot of in-depth conversation with the president, though. Trump's golf conversations go about 7,000 yards long and one inch deep. Often, Trump and his caddy ride in their own cart and will always be way ahead of you, the better to kick, foozle, or throw his ball out of the cabbage.

"It's like a roller coaster ride," says author James Patterson, who belongs to both Trump Westchester and Trump International in West Palm Beach. "He's a good golfer. He's a real golfer. But we rushed around more than I would've loved. We were playing through people all the time. I hate playing through people. You're like, 'Sorry about this. Won't be but a minute. Excuse me.' I don't play well doing that."

Eruzione got to play with him on the day of Barbara Bush's funeral, the one Trump was or wasn't invited to, depending on which network you watch. Eruzione was just standing around the pro shop at Trump Jupiter when the president called up looking to see which celebrities might be hanging around. Trump loves playing with celebrities. David Trout, the Jupiter pro, named Eruzione. "Great!" Trump said.

Eruzione had a ball. "It was great. We played fairly quickly. We went through five or six foursomes." I've been playing golf 45 years and have never played through more than two foursomes in one round in my life. So five or six groups is triple warp speed.

Three and a half hours later—sometimes less—the round will be over and you'll have no idea what he shot or you shot but it'll be fun. I asked Eruzione how Trump played the day he played with him. "I don't really know. We only putted out on a few holes. He had a couple of presidential mulligans. He said that was his right.

He picked up putts. He's the president; he can do whatever he wants to do. We really played fast and then he left. He had to get right out of there and go watch the Barbara Bush service. So I have no idea what he shot. He'd play four or five holes even, then make a double bogey and then he'd pick up. His tee ball was a little erratic that day. He'd push it to the right. He's pretty good, though."

Now he'll invite you to the grill room for lunch. I wasn't with Trump, though, the day I played Bedminster, so I skipped lunch and went straight to the caddyshack.

It's actually not a shack at all, but a stately white one-story cottage near the first tee that's a doppelganger for the Eisenhower cottage at Augusta. Trump hasn't been invited to join Augusta, so perhaps this is his reasonable facsimile. Inside, a dozen guys in white overalls (also very Augusta) were watching a huge TV and eating free cheeseburgers whipped up by the resident caddy/cook, Scotty.

I love caddies because caddies will tell you the truth and use very few words doing it. A buddy of mine played awful one day in Ireland. He hit it all over the map. At the end of 18, he said to his caddy, "What do I owe you?" The caddy scowled at him and said, "A fucking apology."

I sat at the Bedminster caddy house kitchen table and threw out a question to nobody and everybody:

So what's it like working for Trump?

That sat them straight up in their seats.

"No cheating stories!" one caddy hollered out and everybody laughed.

"Mr. Trump is really generous," one caddy began. "Every time he comes in here, [he asks] how we're all doing, are we doing good, stuff like that. And he hands everybody a $100. Guys who aren't here are always like, 'Damn! I missed that?'"

A caddy over by the fridge wrinkled his nose.

FRIDGE CADDY: "Wait. You're saying every single time he comes in here he hands everybody hundreds? Because I've never once seen that."

FIRST CADDY: "Well, okay, not *every* time."

FRIDGE CADDY: "I mean, how many times has he even *been* in here?"

FIRST CADDY: "Well, at least once."

Everybody agreed Trump was a good player, an "8 or 9," they all said, knowing full well that he tells the world he's a 3.

Does he cheat?

There was a lot of sudden interest in birds out the window. One caddy held his hand up while looking me right in the eye. His expression was flat, but his eyes were very wide, like he was about to give me a clue on *Password*.

"Donald Trump never cheats," he said, slowly and sternly.

He stared at me.

Blink. Stare. Blink.

"Ohhh!" I said. "His caddy cheats FOR him?"

The entire room howled. What followed was a dozen or so stories about just HOW he cheats.

- "He's always got four balls in his pocket, if that tells you anything."
- "He foozles his ball on every hole. All 18. I promise you. Every hole."
- "He wants you to throw it out of the woods, kick it out of the rough, fluff up his lie. We all know the deal."

Most of them said they didn't mind doing it but felt a little bad when there was money on the line or a tournament going on.

"I have a friend at his course in Palm Beach," one caddy said, "a really, really good player. He's a +3 or +4 [that means he averages three or four strokes *under par*]. It kills him to do what you gotta do when you caddy for Trump. It absolutely *kills* him."

All the cheating Trump's caddies do for him actually hurts Trump's game. His only real weakness, besides the ethics bypass he seems to have undergone, is chipping around the greens, where he's just awful. That's why his caddies fluff up nasty lies, take his balls out of bunkers, and kick his ball onto the green out of the cabbage. But if you never have those lies, you never learn how to hit them. "Because of the caddies, he never gets to practice those hard shots around the green," says Ned Scherer, who has played with Trump at least 10 times and belongs to both Trump D.C. and Trump Jupiter. "Golf is all about practice, but he never even gets to try them."

Trump's caddy at Bedminster is almost always a very friendly Jamaican gentleman. People like to tell about the time Trump hit one in the pond. Everybody saw it splash a good 30 feet from shore. The Jamaican gentleman was forecaddying. When the group got up to the pond, the caddy says, "Boss, your ball is right here." It was sitting safely on grass. Somebody in the group yelled at the caddy, "What did you do with your mask and flippers?"

Like so much of what happens with Trump, the caddies were revolted by the immorality of the cheating but impressed by the genius of it.

"For a while he kept a can of red spray paint in his cart," one caddy said. "Whenever his ball hit a tree that he didn't think was fair, he'd go up and paint a big X on it. The next day, it was gone."

"That's true!" somebody else yelled. "It's like the mafia with him. You get the red X, you're dead."

It's a great gig, caddying at Bedminster, and none of them want to wreck it, which is why they're smart enough to keep their names out of this. They're also smart enough to keep up with the main two Trump caddy rules.

1. If you're caddying *for* Trump, keep the hell up.

The caddies say his golf cart—the #1—is rigged to go twice as fast as the rest. Keep up with him or put in your application at Chili's. "You gotta run. I mean you gotta sprint. Especially if you're forecaddying. We used to have this guy, he'd come in from 18 with Mr. Trump, run straight into that bathroom, and throw up. But he always made it."

2. If you're caddying *against* Trump, lose.

"Mr. Trump always takes the best caddy," an older caddy explained, "and he makes sure the guy he's playing against gets a shitty caddy or a brand-new caddy. We had this one guy, it was his first week, and it was a match with Mr. Trump and one of our best players versus these two guys from another club. The visitors got the new kid. But somehow, this kid got them around pretty good and it's all tied going into 18. Now, Mr. Trump is fuming. The kid has no idea he's about to get fired. No clue he's got a noose around his neck. But Mr. Trump's partner pulls it out and they end up winning, but, man, that kid came close."

Funny, though, the best Trump story I heard wasn't from a caddy but from a member who came up to me as I was looking at the tournament plaques on the locker room wall. Trump was listed as winner of the "Super Seniors Club Championship" three times, which, naturally, Trump counts in his 18 club championships. Super Seniors is usually defined as age 60 and over. He was also listed as the winner of the "Senior Club Championship" one time—50 and over. But on the regular "Club Championship" plaque, he wasn't listed at all. But there was another plaque, the "Bedminster Member-Member," and Trump's name was on that three times. A "member-member" is a two-man team tournament. It's usually a one-day deal, the team with the lowest bestball score wins.

Anyway, this barrel-chested guy came up to me.

"You know how Donald got one of those?" he said.

No, but I'd sure like to.

"Okay, you'll love this. One year we were playing the Member-Member on the Old Course. But Trump wasn't in it. He and his buddy were just playing by themselves at the New Course. When they were done, he came in to the pro shop and asked what score won the Member-Member. They told him some number, net 61 or something. Whatever. And Trump goes, 'Oh, me and so-and-so played better than that today. So we actually won.' And the pro is like, 'I'm sorry?' And Trump tells them that he and his buddy should be the winners and the guy should put their names on the plaque instead. And that's how he won one of those Member-Members. Can you believe that?"

Yes. Yes, I can.

But you? You should definitely go to lunch with him, because it's the most unforgettable burger you'll ever have.

Take his lunches at Trump Washington. According to a waiter I spoke to there, the Secret Service always puts him at the corner table, a six-top. There are agents everywhere. There's an agent standing in each corner of the grill, too, with more scattered around the restaurant. There's even one with the chef, all morning, to watch where he gets the food and how he cooks it. "Mr. Trump always has a burger, every time," the waiter said. "He also likes to come for breakfast before his round."

Trump will order up a ton of fries, cheeseburgers, maybe some hot dogs, and lots of Diet Cokes. Anybody can come up and sit down. Yes, you heard that right. Anybody can come up to the president's table and have a seat, ask questions, shoot the breeze. Is this a great country or what?

Keep your ears open, because Trump will say nearly anything. It was at a post-round lunch early in his presidency when Trump told a group of Bedminster members the White House was "a fucking dump," a quote that made it into Alan Shipnuck's story on Trump in *Sports Illustrated*, caused a bit of a dustup, and was renounced by Trump in a tweet:

I love the White House, one of the most beautiful buildings (homes) I have ever seen. But Fake News said I called it a dump—TOTALLY UNTRUE

But a source inside Bedminster corroborates it. "This was just after he'd been elected," the source said. "He was having lunch and pontificating on this and that, about Paris (climate change) and how he'd kicked Hillary's ass and just everything. And then he goes, 'I can't believe I gotta live in the White House. What a fucking dump.'"

Keep your head on a swivel, too, because there's always insanity that comes with Trump on a golf day. Remember when Trump greeted 180 Harley Davidson cyclists as part of a bizarre pro-Trump anti-Harley Davidson rally? That happened outside the clubhouse at Bedminster. Remember that whole incident when a Breitbart reporter alleged that Trump campaign manager Corey Lewandowski grabbed her violently by the arm while she was trying to ask Trump a question? That happened at Trump Jupiter. Remember all those Cabinet-post interviewees who kept pouring in and out of meetings with Trump? That happened a lob wedge away from the first tee at Trump Bedminster.

Also, as long as you're on property, would you keep an eye out for the famous painting?

It's of Trump. It's six feet tall and was won by Melania at a charity auction for $20,000 (outbidding LPGA star Paula Creamer). It was one of those speed paintings. You know, it takes the guy six minutes and you think he's terrible and then he flips it right side up and there's—Jimi Hendrix! Except this one, painted in

September of 2016 by Michael Israel, was of Trump. The problem was Trump paid for it with $10,000 out of the Trump Foundation, according to the New York Attorney General's office, which is very illegal. If you buy a painting with charity money, it has to be used for charitable purposes—like for the wall of a hospital. But Melania bought it and hung it at Doral, according to the New York Attorney General's office.

There's another famous Trump painting that was never painted at all but still caused some teeth gnashing. After Trump won the election, three members of Winged Foot—where Trump has belonged since 1969—wanted to honor their member/president with a huge painting, to be hung in the clubhouse. "Three members out of 900, by the way," says Thomas Leslie, Winged Foot's president. "They wrote a letter to me saying they thought it was appropriate that the club put up a painting of Mr. Trump now that he was president." Leslie said thanks but no thanks. "I said that without taking any kind of political view on this, we only hang pictures of golfers who've won major championships here or those who were pros here." Left unsaid was that with the Men's U.S. Open coming to Winged Foot in 2020, the less ammo you can give the protesters, the better.

Okay. It's time to say goodbye. But before you go, look around for the famous American Academy of Hospitality Sciences Five-Star Diamond Award plaques every Trump club usually has. I've probably seen them at five different Trump courses.

These plaques are quite a rare honor—"another feather in our cap," as Trump told Mar-a-Lago members in an email once. Except the American Academy of Hospitality Sciences isn't really an academy and it isn't a science. It's just a guy named Joey (No Socks) Cinque and his secretary/girlfriend (No Nylons?) working out of Joey's apartment in New York.

Joey No Socks is quite a character. *New York* magazine says he survived a mob hit and was friends with mob capo John Gotti. New York police nabbed him selling stolen paintings and sculpture, to which Joey pleaded guilty but served no time. After his conviction, Joey bounced around until he came up with this academy beauty and started handing out these awards. Lo and behold, he struck up a friendship with Trump. Along the way, Trump has been named as a trustee, along with three Trump staffers, Trump's two sons, plus Joey's gal, and labor leader Ed Malloy, according to the *Chicago Tribune*. That could win you a lot of five-star diamond awards.

JOEY NO SOCKS: OK, this meeting will come to order. First item of business: who should get our famed American Academy of Hospitality Sciences Five-Star Diamond Award this month? The chair recognizes Mr. Trump.

TRUMP: I name Mr. Donald Trump!

DONALD JR.: I second it!

JOEY NO SOCKS: Done!

As of November 2017, former White House press secretary Anthony Scaramucci and Trump Bedminster General Manager David Schutzenhofer were still listed as "trustees."

Joey No Socks even stood next to Trump at his big 2017 New

Year's Eve election-win party at Mar-a-Lago. "There's nobody like him," Trump said back in 2009. "He's a special guy."

When asked about socializing with a convicted mobster, Trump said, "Hey, if a guy's going to give you an award, you take it. You don't tend to look up his whole life story."

Right. Why would a president want to do that?

Anyway, now it's *really* time for you to go. Hope you didn't steal anything. That's Joey No Socks in your rearview mirror.

9

MO TRUMP MO PROBLEMS

I like having friends, but I like having enemies more.
—DONALD J. TRUMP

THERE WAS ONCE A sleepy little town about an hour south of Los Angeles perched on palm-sweaty cliffs overlooking the blue Pacific called Rancho Palos Verdes. It was a wonderful place to take a nap. Most of the bars closed at 11:30—in the morning. With mostly rich, retired, Republican seniors living in it, Rancho Palos Verdes was about the most peaceful burg you might ever find in all of southern California.

Was, that is, until Donald Trump showed up.

It all started with a thunderous roar. "It sounded like this massive incredible rumbling," remembers singer Tom Sullivan, who lives there. "The ground was shaking under us."

But it wasn't an earthquake. It was the sound of a golf hole sliding into the sea. It was June 2, 1999, six weeks before the much-ballyhooed Pete Dye–designed Ocean Trails Golf Club was supposed to open. Most of the 496-yard, cliff-hanging 18th hole was just…gone. The project built by two brothers—Ken and Bob Zuckerman—was now officially screwed.

Eventually, they'd file for bankruptcy. A few years after that, riding to the rescue, came the new buyer, Donald J. Trump.

The town was delighted. This was 2002 and Trump wasn't a TV star then. All they knew was that he was an East Coast tycoon who jetted around on a 737 with his name on it, had fine spun-red hair, and was usually standing next to his latest knockout wife. They also knew he had a very thick checkbook and a love of golf and would probably rebuild the course in a swanky way. They immediately invited him to town to celebrate this wonderful new relationship. Only Rancho Palos Verdes had no idea they'd just gotten in the ring with a brawler.

Even as a kid, Donald Trump relished a good fight, sought them out, thrived on them. He was that very bad combination: very big and thin-skinned. He'd pull girls' hair. He'd pound his baseball bat into the ground. He'd bully smaller kids. "In the second grade I actually gave a teacher a black eye," he wrote in *The Art of the Deal.* "I didn't think he knew anything about music and I almost got expelled." He spent so much time in detention, he got the nickname "DT." Worse, no matter how much trouble he got in, Double Down always came back for twice as much.

At 13, his parents sent him to New York Military Academy, hoping it might smooth him out. It didn't. Donald came out of military school fists up. His thirst for scrapping can't be quenched. "My rule is when attacked, fire back 10 times harder," he once said. And he's not talking about for a while. He's talking forever.

Trump likes talking tough. Likes to tweet about kicking Joe Biden's ass. Likes to poo-poo NFL anti-spearing rules to protect players' brains as "ruining the game." Likes telling 1980 U.S. Olympic hockey hero Mike Eruzione that he liked the NHL better "when they didn't wear helmets." (To which Eruzione replied, "Without helmets, a lot of players you watch would be in the hospital today.")

Fistfights in golf are rare, but Trump likes telling about the time he punched a guy out at Winged Foot. "It was this big handsome asshole," Trump told me. "And he was just being a complete jerk! So I sink this putt on the ninth hole to win the match and then I turn and just coldcock him, just knock him out right there on the green!... They ended up suspending both of us. I was back off suspension after two weeks and he never got back in."

A couple questions: (a) How do you win a match on the ninth hole? (b) If Trump just suddenly swung and punched, why did the other guy get booted? (c) And why for good?

Besides, that's not how some people at Winged Foot tell it. "First of all, Trump is not well liked at Winged Foot," says member Bill Fugazy, who has known Trump for years and whose late father also knew him there. "He's just bad news to be around, a weird guy. It's hard for him to get a game. So when it happened, he was playing by himself.

"The turn there is on 10, not 9. So he goes into the bar to have a quick soda, then goes to the 11th hole. But the guys ahead of him were just getting on the tee. One of them goes, 'Donald, what do you think you're doing?' Trump goes, 'Playing through.' The guy goes, 'Yeah? Well, usually you ask permission for that. That's kinda rude.' Words were exchanged. Trump goes, 'Get the fuck out of my way.' This guy goes, 'Who you talking to?' Trump shoves him and leaves the course. He was brought in and suspended. The other guy wasn't suspended. Why should he be? He didn't do anything."

So no punch-out?

"Who's he gonna punch?" Fugazy says. "He's got tiny spongey hands. He couldn't punch anybody."

As Trump got older and started making too many millions to go around punching people, he decided suing them in court was the next best thing. It's another chance to fight and win. Even better, if he loses, he can always say it was rigged, or the judge was crooked, or Hispanic. Or he can settle and not have to admit he lost at all.

Trump loves suing like he loves red ties. He'll sue over anything: flagpoles, trees, hedges, fences, berms, neighbors' yards, roads, streets, sidewalks, taxes, fees, airplane noise, helicopter pads, property lines, university scams, water, drainage, unpaid bills, half-paid bills, too much rent, not enough rent, stolen deposits, zoning, the environment, courses he's built, courses he didn't, deals he made, deals he didn't, paintings of himself, donations, schools, his announced net worth, and his *actual* net worth. He's sued friends, enemies, partners, and rivals. Trump has sued and been sued by just about everybody. According to *USA Today*, as of mid-2016, Trump had been part of more than 3,500 lawsuits in his life. That's almost 50 lawsuits a year, since birth.

Don't most sports billionaires tangle themselves up in that many lawsuits? Isn't that just part of the game at that level? "Not me," says Mark Cuban. "In my whole life, I've been sued twice, I think."

Poor little Rancho Palos Verdes had no idea about any of that when Trump showed up to their packed town hall to celebrate this new and imperfect union of town and golf course. Trump walked to the podium to cheers and immediately gave the citizens a hint of the fuckery to come.

He started with a reference to the last course he'd rebuilt—Trump Westchester in New York. "If you had called the mayor of Briarcliff Manor five years ago and asked him, 'Whaddya think of Trump?' his answer probably wouldn't have been not so great [*sic*]. We were fighting them really hard. But if you call him now, he'd say it's the finest relationship they've ever had....Everybody in the town loves us."

That would've been news that day to then-mayor of Briarcliff Manor, Bill Vescio, considering Trump has barely ever stopped suing his 38,000-person town, or insulting him on Twitter, or telling people not to vote for him since the day he bought the place. As I write this, Trump is suing the town again, this time over taxes.

That moment at the podium in Rancho Palos Verdes was the start of 16 years of chaos—Trump versus Rancho Palos Verdes, a 10-round knockout fight.

Round 1: Trump v. Schools

Turns out, much to Trump's surprise, he hadn't quite bought the entire golf course. Some of it—basically the 15th hole—still belonged to the Rancho Palos Verdes (RPV) school district. Without it, Trump would have a back eight.

Trump flipped. He started calling the superintendent of schools at the time, Ira Toibin, to tell him how unfair it was and how they'd hidden this information from him and how he might sue and how they needed to fix this immediately, if not sooner. He'd call Toibin at home, work, everywhere. "I must've had six personal phone calls with Mr. Trump," says Toibin, a very buttoned-up sort of man who, at press time, was again the RPV school superintendent. "He hadn't read the paperwork. It was such a lucrative deal, he hadn't really read it. He didn't know who we were at all. He kept wanting to negotiate [a buyout] with me. But I kept saying, 'I don't negotiate, Mr. Trump. I have our attorney do that for us.'"

That attorney would become a pain in Trump's famous neck. He was the school district's very determined Milan Smith, who wound up publicly calling Trump "arrogant" and "pompous."

"I have never had any contact with any human being who appears to be so self-absorbed and so impressed with himself," Smith told a tiny beach paper called *The Easy Reader.* "He's kind of like a big bag of wind."

One time, Trump got up at an RPV town meeting and called Smith an "obnoxious asshole." In this sedate little town, these were words that you just never heard. Wait until the book clubs heard about it! But calling Smith an "obnoxious asshole" turned out to be a very bad idea for Trump, since The Obnoxious Asshole is now a federal judge on the Ninth Circuit Court of Appeals, the body that overturned Trump's first Muslim-country travel ban.

Trump's complaint was that Smith wanted too much for the missing land—$5 million. Trump wanted to pay $1 million. Smith was as immovable as an Easter Island statue. So Trump kept calling Toibin.

"He'd call and yell at me, using a lot of swear words. [Toibin doesn't swear, so you'll have to fill in with your imagination.] 'You _____ guys are trying to rip me off! It's not worth _____ $5 million! Come to New York and ____ negotiate with me!' I kept telling him, 'Donald, this money will go to kids' educations, to kids' facilities. Plus, the state will match it. So it's $10 million for the kids. Think of it as a donation."

"This is 'Trump-change' for him," Smith said, knowing perhaps that nobody can run a golf course shaped like a donut. In the end, Trump paid the $5 million. But he never forgot it.

Round 2: Trump v. Patriotism

Trying to stiff school kids will get you some nasty PR in a small town, but Trump bounced back with a great idea: patriotism. Trump is very good at clubbing people over the head with his patriotism. (*See: NFL.*) He immediately put up a 70-foot flagpole in front of his clubhouse with a flag that could nicely cover Mount Rushmore. Giant flag poles are a standard trick Trump uses at his clubs. When he first tried it, at Mar-a-Lago, he complained that he absolutely had to have a massive flagpole because, as his attorneys wrote, a smaller one "would fail to appropriately express the magnitude of Donald J. Trump's...patriotism." Just so you know, Donald J. Trump's patriotism is exactly 100 feet high. One hundred and ten feet? No.

Rancho Palos Verdes was almost entirely Republican, but this mother of all flagpoles was just way too much and well over the city's allowed limit. The city told him to cut it down to 26 feet or get rid of it. Trump refused. It went to the city council for debate.

That sound you just heard was the trap door slamming. Trump ran, not walked, to the papers to complain that the city was infringing on his patriotism. *What kind of country is this where they make a man feel bad for putting up an American flag?* And it's true, nobody is more patriotic than Donald Trump, except for perhaps when there's a military draft going on. The city looked bad. The town split in two over it, with the giant-flag crowd far outweighing the but-that's-ridiculous crowd. They let Trump keep the pole, and the flag, just like it was.

Only RPV city councilman Steve Wolowicz, a lifetime Republican, seemed to get what was happening. "I have to offer congratulations to all of us," he said, "for providing the very type of publicity that a real estate developer seeks."

Round 3: Trump v. Laundry

It started with Tiger Woods. In 2007, the actor Michael Douglas was holding an annual celebrity pro-am tournament and schmoozefest at Trump Los Angeles, and they said Woods was going to show up. That's when Trump took a look at the distant houses 360 yards from the tees at his practice range and decided they were very ugly. He had a long row of 10-foot-high ficus trees planted in front of them so nobody would have to look at the houses while hitting their practice shots—not Tiger, not Douglas, not Catherine Zeta-Jones, nobody. The problem with the trees is that they blocked the homeowners' views of the ocean, a view they'd paid dearly to have. Trump's people said it was just temporary, but long after the tournament, the ficus trees were still there.

Complaints started pouring into the city. The council decided to meet with Trump about it—at the "ugly" houses themselves. Yes, Trump would be going *inside* these homes.

The whole gaggle walked from the Trump Los Angeles driving range to the eye-offending abodes and the view-blocking trees. Along the way, Trump called these very expensive, ocean-front, gated homes "horrendous" and "ugly" and "awful." Then he walked into the backyard of the one belonging to a resident named Jessica Leeds. There were towels drying on the balcony railing from a recent trip to the beach. With Ms. Leeds standing there, Trump said, "Your house looks like shit." Also: "This house is ugly. My customers shouldn't have to look at your ugly house." I don't know about you, but if I ever talked that way to somebody inside their house, my mom would've whacked me with a frying pan. Yet nobody stopped Trump, nobody upbraided him, nobody made him apologize. It was all too awkward for polite little Rancho Palos Verdes.

They said a lot more at the next council meeting. One man got up at the meeting and said, "Since purchasing this property, the Trump Organization has done what they want, how they want and when they want it with complete disregard for its governing authorities."

The council voted unanimously to force Trump to take down the trees. Even Trump's Winnebago full of lawyers couldn't fix it. Trump lost and issued his standard quote for such occasions: "We've been treated very unfairly."

The whole tree trick is SOP for Trump golf. At his Doral resort, more than 2,500 residents complained that Trump had put up high trees that blocked their views. Some of them got so mad they started ripping them apart at night. Trump sued five middle-class Doral homeowners who bordered his property for $15,000 each.

"There are behaviors in people's backyards that are inconsistent with a world-class set of golf courses like Donald Trump is attempting to create," a Trump spokesman said. That must've been a great surprise to the neighbors. They had no idea they were part of a world-class set of golf courses. Come to think of it, they weren't. They had zero to do with it. Most of them didn't even play golf. What were their horrible behaviors? "Playing music, drinking alcohol, and hanging out undergarments on their clotheslines."

The nerve.

Round 4: Trump v. Dead People

The way Trump sees it, you can't very well play Trump National Golf Club Los Angeles and drink Trump bottled water and buy Trump golf balls unless you drive up Donald Trump National

Drive first. He wanted to rename the road leading to his club from Ocean Trails Drive to that name, but the city had rules about that kind of thing. You had to be dead to get a street named after you, and by all accounts, Trump was not dead. Trump sued, because Trump is very serious about putting his name on things.

The squabble over the street was stirred into a whole other bubbling cauldron of trouble...

Round 5: Trump v. Homes

Trump had a desire to start building lots of homes on his property, which wasn't part of the deal. The city rejected him. Trump sued for $100 million, accusing the city council of fraud and violating his due process. The council, exhausted and Trump-weary, decided to try a new tactic. Give in on half his demands and hold fast to the ones that really matter, and maybe, somehow, he'll take that as a win. On this case, he did. He got his eponymous road, but lost on the houses.

Round 6: Trump v. Time

When you go to any Trump golf property, you'll notice there are always a gazillion framed articles and magazine covers about... (wait for it)...Trump. But not long after Trump Los Angeles opened, a *Washington Post* reporter noticed something odd at the club. There was a *Time* magazine Man of the Year cover with Trump's picture on it. Except it was fake. The date on it was March 1, 2009, a date *Time* didn't publish a magazine. The closest magazine to that date had Kate Winslet on the cover. Trump had never been Man of the Year. It seemed very unfair. He tweeted:

> **The Time Magazine list of the 100 Most Influential People is a joke and stunt of a magazine that will, like Newsweek, soon be dead. Bad list!**

Once the fake Man of the Year cover was discovered at Trump Los Angeles, people started reporting fake Man of the Year covers at other courses—five of his clubs in all, including clubs in Scotland and Ireland. Trump's people ended up taking them all down, but why? Shouldn't winning 18 fake club championships automatically win you fake *Time* Man of the Year?

Round 7: Trump v. Taxes

Some people like to drive to Cape Canaveral for rocket launches. I like to watch Trump tell people what he's put into his golf courses. It's classic Trump Bump.

It usually starts at $100 million. "I'm putting $100 million into this course," he'll say. "By the time I'm done, it'll be the most expensive course in the world." Then it will balloon. Soon it will be "$150 million," then "$200 million," and eventually it'll top out at "$250 million," although he once said he put "$325 million" into Trump Aberdeen. If you paved every fairway in gold, and lined the cups with diamonds, you couldn't spend $325 million on a golf course.

At Trump Los Angeles, Trump worked his way up to "$264

million" sunk into the course. That's a lie so full of hot air it could float the *Queen Mary*. Course appraiser Larry Hirsh actually LOL'd when I told him the $264 million figure. "I guess anything is possible," he said. "But for somebody to put $264 million into a golf course would be a very, very big challenge." Saying you put $264 million into a golf course is like saying you went to the fridge and made yourself a $50,000 sandwich. We know it's a lie because not long after Trump announced the $264 million figure, his lawyers were suing the L.A. County Assessor's office for its assessment of the course. They said it was only worth $10 million. So, Trump was only off by $254 million.

Round 8: Trump v. Dye

The only problem with Trump Los Angeles is that it sucks. It's a monotonous layout. It's back and forth, forth and back, every hole but one running parallel to the ocean, every ball bouncing toward the ocean, every putt breaking toward the ocean, until, eventually, you want to jump in the ocean. And that doesn't even count the three horrid waterfalls it opened with. Once you play it, you'll see why the LPGA only played one year on it and bolted.

"I only played 14 holes of it," says Scottish golf architect David McLay Kidd, who designed Bandon Dunes. "I got so tediously bored that I walked in. It's narrow. It's blind. It's contrived.... Donald Trump's answer is always spend more money, build more, more cart paths, more waterfalls. Sometimes what's required is restraint."

That might be why Pete Dye, the original designer, made Trump take his name off the course.

"I met with Mr. Trump and we discussed his branding and redesign concepts for Ocean Trails," says Perry Dye, Pete's son. "We 'agreed to disagree'—as is now very hard to do with President Trump....He wanted waterfalls....We felt that...was unnecessary, as all 18 holes already look at the Pacific Ocean and Catalina Island."

It doesn't help, either, that a single round at Trump Los Angeles costs $300.

Trump is right though: The views of the Pacific are incredible. Luckily, the California Coastal Commission forced Trump to keep the hiking trails in and around the course open, so you can see it all for free.

Round 9: Trump v. Charity

On the official website for Trump Los Angeles, there used to be a page telling you how Trump Los Angeles had given over $5 million to charity since their opening. There was a list of over 200 causes it had donated to, and, hey, wouldn't the world be a better place if we all opened our hearts and wallets like Trump L.A.?

The only problem was they actually hadn't donated anywhere near $5 million. In a lengthy investigation, NPR could only document $800,000 in donations, and most of that was free rounds and free brunches.

In fact, of the 200 organizations the club listed, 17 said they couldn't find any record of a donation of any kind from the club, and 26 others couldn't be proven one way or the other. Many of them weren't even charities at all, like the LAPD Homicide Bureau.

Here you go, boys—free fingerprint kits. On us!

Some didn't exist at all—Downed Officers Fund, Sing for the Heart, Simply Not Simple. Those were listed, but they were all fake. So somebody was zooming somebody.

The Trump Organization did not return calls to NPR or to me on this subject, but did take out the bogus $5 million claim and 86'd the list.

Round 10: Trump v. Women

Like his golf courses and clubhouses, Trump wants everything to be a 10, including the women he employs at them, according to a lawsuit filed by women who worked at his course in Rancho Palos Verdes.

According to them, Trump insisted on "good-looking women" to hold down his hostess stands and his waitress jobs. "I had witnessed Donald Trump tell managers many times while he was visiting the club that restaurant hostesses were 'not pretty enough' and that they should be fired and replaced with more attractive women," swore Hayley Strozier, who was the director of catering at the club until 2008. That was backed up by restaurant manager Sue Kwiatkowski, who said that one time, he took her aside and said, "I want you to get some good-looking hostesses here. People like to see good-looking people when they come in."

He likes them to be young, too, according to Lucy Messer-schmidt, a then-hostess who said she got yanked from the schedule whenever Trump was on the premises. Stacia Solis testified that younger, prettier waitresses would be assigned to serve Trump's table, even if they weren't the best. One male employee testified he never saw a male waiter serve Trump. One female supervisor refused to fire a female employee even though her boss said Trump wanted her gone because she was "fat."

Trump settled that mess for $475,000, though he admitted no guilt.

So, 15 years later, after all the lawsuits, nastiness, and Excedrin headaches, how does the very Republican enclave of Rancho Palos Verdes, California, feel *now* about Donald Trump?

Well, in 2008, it voted for John McCain, in 2012 for Mitt Romney, and in 2016, overwhelmingly, for Hillary Clinton.

10

ONE GOOD PUNCH

My whole life is about winning. I don't lose.
—Donald J. Trump

FOR DECADES NOW, THE golf world has known something about Trump that the rest of the world is just finding out. Yes, Trump is a very big dealmaker, but he's an even bigger deal breaker. Doesn't matter what he's said to the press or what he's signed or what he's shaken on, when it comes time to pay up, he can flip like a weathervane.

That moment will be the crucible for you. That's when you'll find out if you can be shaken down or find the guts to stand up to him. Whether you're the chancellor of Germany or a wallpaper guy, that moment with Trump can make or break your company, your career, your life. It's happened in golf a hundred times. Some rise to it, others get buried by it.

At Trump Westchester, the architect who designed the

55,000-square-foot clubhouse, Andrew Tesoro, had it happen to him, and it threatened to kick a very big hole in his life.

Tesoro was a 50-something architect on Columbus Circle in New York City, a single dad of an adopted son. At first, he thought it was kind of cool to be working for Trump. "I can remember one time, I brought my son out with me to the course," Tesoro said. "He was maybe five. Donald saw Victor and was kind enough to give him a lesson. He put a little kiddie club in his hand—you know, a cut-down regular golf club for kids—and showed him how to swing it. Victor was so excited. But then Trump took the club back. Victor started crying. He wanted to swing the club. I tried to tell him, 'He was only loaning the club to you, son'—but five-year-olds aren't that good at understanding loans. It really irritated Trump, my son crying. He turned away from us, handed the club to one of his lackeys, and walked off. I learned that about him. He's not patient with kids."

Pretty soon, Tesoro noticed that Trump wasn't all that patient with bills either. Trump kept paying $10,000 invoices with checks for $6,000. Tesoro just figured it was some kind of accounting system he didn't understand and kept working. "Many people told me, 'Inflate your bills because Trump will chisel you.' I didn't do that because I'm a fair and honest guy. My way of doing business is to treat people with decency and figure they'll treat you that way back."

Big mistake.

By the time he got to the end of the job, Trump still owed him well over $100,000 in unpaid bills. Tesoro went to Trump's main point man on the golf project and complained. The man told him to come to the clubhouse the next day and meet with two of the managers Tesoro knew well and they'd settle up. "They'll chisel you down, but they'll settle," the guy said.

So the next day, Tesoro came by himself and walked into the clubhouse he'd designed. But it wasn't just Tesoro meeting with two staffers. There were 40 people in the lobby. All the vendors were there, from the tile guy, to the electrician, to the landscaper. "And it wasn't two people we were going to meet with, it was 15 administrators and lawyers, all there to gang up on the little guys."

Tesoro put his name on the clipboard and waited. At last, he was called into a big boardroom with all the suits around a big table, 30 eyebrows furrowed. He took his chair. They got out a big stack of papers and went through all his bills, one by one. "I remember one bill was for something like $2,147 for bathrooms. The guy looks at it and goes, 'Well, you should've known a bill for that much wasn't going to please him.'"

Hey Visa, why'd you send my husband a bill for $2,147? You must've known that wasn't going to please him.

In the end, Trump's people offered him 40 cents on the dollar—$56,000 on a bill of over $141,000—take it or leave it. They said he could sue, sure, but they'd tie him up in court for seven or eight years and he still might not get it. Welcome to Trumpland. Tesoro said he needed time to think. He went home and stewed about it. He wondered how he could keep his business going if he was fighting Donald J. Trump in court for the next seven years.

"I didn't want to fight. I wanted to be an architect." A few days later, he sent Trump a bill for a flat $50,000. He still didn't get paid.

This time Tesoro went straight to Trump himself. Trump greeted him in his Trump Tower office like a returning astronaut. "How's the best architect in the world?" Trump said with a big handshake and smile. "Have a seat!"

Finally, Tesoro asked him, flat out, "Why don't you pay me?" Trump explained to Tesoro how the project cost too much and took too long. Tesoro wondered how that was his problem. Trump stood up, offered his handshake, and said he'd give him $25,000, and otherwise, he could go talk to Bernie, his lawyer, down the hall.

In the end, Tesoro took the $25,000—18% of what he was owed.

"I got snookered," Tesoro says. "I'm pretty savvy, but I got conned and snookered. When I see [Senator] Lindsey Graham and members of Congress kissing his ass over stuff they know isn't right for the country, I don't blame them. He makes fools of people. I know how persuasive that man is now."

It was all rancid water under the bridge until Tesoro was taking Victor to school one day and a mother said, "You should go public with your story." Tesoro wanted no part of it, but she kept bugging him. Finally, he agreed. Next thing you know, he was on a "Hillary Clinton for President" TV ad—the architect who got stiffed by the Republican nominee for president.

"I got thousands of emails, Facebook comments, phone calls from strangers, everything, mostly supportive and sympathetic," Tesoro says. "Maybe 10% were like, 'Oh, you were probably trying to rip him off.' That's what some people think. People would call me to say they were still going to vote for Trump. Some called to say they weren't going to vote for Trump. But I wasn't paid a dime to do it and, what's more, I never got an ounce of work out of it."

The money Trump shorted him not only robbed young Victor of money that would've sent him to a school he wanted to go to—Yale or Princeton—but time, too. "He [Victor] didn't get much attention from me through all of this," Tesoro says, a little regretfully. "I spent so much time trying to fight Trump that I had a terrible year in business and didn't get to pay much attention to my son in his last year of high school. But Victor understands. He gets it. At one point, he said, 'You know, Dad, that Trump guy is kind of like Hitler.' And I said, 'No. That's taking it too far.' But now, after seeing him as president, I think my son might be closer to the truth than I thought."

Then there was a young lawyer named Brad Edwards.

In a tiny office, in a gentrifying section of Fort Lauderdale, Edwards was handed a case that made his eyes bug. It involved Trump Jupiter golf club and, to Edwards, it seemed too good to be true.

It all started when Trump bought the debt-plagued Ritz-Carlton Jupiter golf resort and transformed it into Trump National Golf Club Jupiter. It was a killer buy—$5 million for a nice Jack Nicklaus course and clubhouse with 400 members in America's ritziest golf address.

There was only one tricky part—Trump also got $51 million in an odd kind of debt—deposits the club owed to members, who had each put up whopping initiation fees, some up to $200,000, for an equity membership. (An equity club means the members own it. A nonequity club means the developer owns it.) That means they could get their money back when they quit, as long as there was a buyer to take their place, and there was always going to be a buyer, everybody figured. After all, it's Jupiter.

Now that $51 million is absolutely untouchable to the new owner of an equity club. You can put it in a CD and get 1% or 2% interest, but you are not ethically allowed to speculate with it, use it for your own purposes, borrow it, spend it, use it for condos, put it into your jet, nothing. Hands off, as written in the contract.

Except in TrumpWorld.

In his first big meeting with his Jupiter members, Trump held a town hall, laid on the charm, and fired up the boaster oven. He said he was going to create the "best club in America" on the "best piece of land" in all of Florida, and pretty soon you'll be at the most "sought-after" so on and so forth. Oh, and one more little thing, you're not going to get your initiation fee back. I'm putting all $51 million into the course.

That one sentence made the members sit up straight in their chairs. There were about 150 in that room who were already on the list to sell their memberships. They'd signed a deal saying they could. And now this billionaire was just going to walk away with their $51 million?

It got worse. Trump then wrote everybody a letter: "If you

choose to remain on the resignation list—you're out [of the club]." Not only were you out—meaning you couldn't play golf at the club, eat at the club, drink at the club, set foot on the grounds, or even look over the hedges—but you'd STILL have to pay your monthly dues until your membership could be replaced. Most private golf clubs add 25 or 30 new members a year, so that meant the last guy on that list might wait five years to get his money back and still have to pay his dues every month—for nothing.

No way that would stand up in court. It was just an empty threat. They had a written contract, and nowhere did it say they were out of the club for getting on the resignation list. Who would be scared by that?

Answer: Most of them.

The thought of having to sue Donald Trump and his small stadium of lawyers scared the pee out of them. Most went along with Trump's shakedown. They forked over their huge deposits and joined Hurricane Trump.

The remaining 65 lawyered up in the form of a class-action suit brought by Edwards, who not only didn't flinch at having to go up against Trump, he licked his lips.

"I try a lot of cases," Edwards said. "A lot of really difficult cases. But it's rare when you get such a slam-dunk. It just looked—impossible to lose."

Trump's coterie of lawyers tried the usual stall tactics, paper threats, and time-wasting motions. None of it worked. These 65 members had enough money they weren't going to run and hide. It went to a hearing. Edwards flew to New York and deposed pre-president Trump, who said, basically, "Nope. I'm reading

the contract differently. I read these deposits as nonrefundable."
This would be like looking at a cow and saying, "Nope. I see a
chicken." How was that possible when it read right in the contract that they got their money back?

"I really don't know," Edwards says.

He deposed Eric Trump, the titular president of the Trump
Organization, who said no, no, no, he hadn't revoked their membership, that they were still allowed to use the club. That was not
true. They all had emails from the club telling them they couldn't
be on the property. Their gate transponders were turned off. Their
head pro told them they couldn't play the course. The only part
of the club they still had access to was their monthly bill. Besides,
Eric's father had already said in deposition that these members
were banned. He described them as "angry people."

Donald reasoned that these members couldn't be around
because, "You're probably not going to be a very good club member. You're not going to be so happy." Apparently, seeing somebody else walking around with $200,000 of your money puts
people in a bad mood.

With all those emails and letters as evidence, Trump was
deader than Bob Hope on this case, and yet he kept fighting. But
why? For a lousy $6 million in dues? When he'd already pock-
eted $45 million in one meeting? That's a pretty good deal, right?

Nope. Good was not good enough for Trump.

Edwards didn't just beat him. He beat him twice. A judge
ruled in February 2017, and again on appeal in January 2018,
that Trump owed the members $4.7 million in dues, plus interest
and legal fees, for a total of $5.4 million. That's not a settlement.

Edwards won a verdict. A young lawyer from a tiny firm next to a taco stand in Fort Lauderdale had just won $5.4 million from the standing president of the United States.

"In the long run, though, Trump had already won," Edwards says, looking back on it all. "He bought this gorgeous club for $5 million. He snapped his fingers and turned $45 million of debt into an asset. It was a great business move. But he just wouldn't quit. And it just taught everybody that even when there's a class of people who were right—and they were clearly right—Trump is a fighter who's gonna fight to the very bitter end, no matter what. You don't just have to beat him, you have to beat him three or four times. You have to keep beating him even as he's laying on the ground because he'll get up and fight some more. The guy will never, ever quit."

Meet Juan Carlos Enriquez.

The bulk of the painting for Trump's re-do of the Doral golf resort in Miami was done by his small mom-and-pop business, The Paint Spot, run by Enriquez and his family. It was a monster job, worth well into six figures.

When he was done, Trump still owed him the final payment, about $30,000. It didn't come and it kept not coming. Enriquez wore out the little door on his mailbox looking for it. Two years went by—no $30,000. You think when Trump talked about the Forgotten Man, he meant Enriquez?

Now, Trump could find $30,000 in the cushions of his 757, but for Enriquez, that was a big chunk of his yearly gross. It was an eight-month job and people had to get paid. "I got three girls, a wife, 10 employees, my brother. I had to get my money," says Enriquez, the son of Cuban immigrants. "People who don't pay leave a bad taste in my mouth."

But Trump wouldn't cough it up. "I've paid enough," Trump told him.

Dear First National,

Stop sending me notices on my car loan. I've paid enough.

Enriquez offered to settle for $26,000. "I don't settle," Trump said.

So the painter took a big gulp and sued Donald J. Trump, soon to be president of the United States.

"I mean, if you're right, you're right," Enriquez says. "So I was 95% sure I was going to win. But the lawsuit kept dragging on and on. The legal bills grew to be 10 times the disputed amount. If I lost, I was going to have to close up shop. It would've been over $400,000. Where am I gonna get $400,000?"

Finally, in 2017, after three years, Enriquez won. Naturally, Trump's lawyers appealed. More sleepless months. Finally, Trump lost the appeal, too, and Enriquez pocketed well over $300,000, most of which went to his lawyer.

But get this. In between, Enriquez actually voted for Trump. "Hey, business and politics are two different things," he says. "I think he's doing what he said he was going to do."

Painters weren't the only people who were stiffed at Doral. There were also the 48 servers who worked a Passover event there and were stiffed between $800 and $3,000 each for overtime. Trump, who "never settles," settled.

"That's nothing new," says former Palm Beach County commissioner Shelley Vana. "We heard of so many vendors who said he didn't pay them. Everybody was saying it. 'Watch out. He doesn't pay his vendors. Be careful.'"

Trump even tried to stiff a guy who made a $1 million hole in one. At a charity tournament at Trump Westchester, a Wall Street tycoon named Marty Greenberg stepped to a tee box that was advertising a $1 million prize to anybody that made an ace there. Greenberg did it. Except Trump's insurance company said, "Nope. The hole had to be at least 150 yards. It was 139." They refused to pay. Trump refused to pay. Greenberg sued. Trump settled for $158,000.

This is where it gets worse. Trump still wouldn't pay it. Instead, he paid it out of the Donald J. Trump Foundation account. What does the Trump Foundation have to do with this, you ask? Absolutely nothing. That was self-dealing and illegal and incurred the Trumps a fat fine, on top of the $158,000, and a few years later, became one of the reasons the Trump Foundation was shut down for good by the New York Attorney General's Office.

But surely lots of golf course/real estate tycoons must have to stop payment and sue constantly, right? With so many contractors to deal with?

"Never," says David Southworth, an American golf course developer in the same league with Trump. "Not once."

Not once? In how many years?

"Twenty-seven," he says. "We've never not paid someone. We've never stiffed anyone. We've certainly had discussions over time with people, we've never just stopped paying them."

Have you ever heard of any other developer doing it?

"No," he says. "But I've been hearing that about Donald for a long time. There must be some merit to it. I hear it enough."

Mike Meldman is on Trump's level. He's the owner of Discovery Land Company, a fantabulous collection of more than 20 fun, unusual, and hip golf courses where rock music is played at the practice range, the snack shack might be a surfboard with legs, and a tequila shot comes just before your tee shot on 18. Places like Gozzer Ranch in Idaho (Wayne Gretzky is a member), Madison Club in La Quinta, California (John Elway), and El Dorado in Cabo San Lucas (George Clooney and Cindy Crawford). Not only does he always pay up, but sometimes he forgets to *stop* paying. His golf-architect bonuses are happy legend. Tom Fazio completely stopped working for Trump a long time ago, but he almost never turns down Meldman. Fazio has a set handshake deal with him: $1.5 million to design a course in the U.S., $3 million to design one out of the U.S., and zero interference from the boss. No muss, no fuss, no weekends.

(The first time Meldman met Trump, he was introduced by Fazio. Trump was just starting to get into golf development. The ever-needling Fazio said, "Donald, this is Mike Meldman, the Donald Trump of golf. This is who you think you are and who you wanna be. But you'll never be him.")

So, Mike Meldman, in your 30-plus years of building golf resorts, have you ever stopped paying anybody?

"No, not once. Not ever."

Ever sue or been sued?

"Maybe . . . twice?"

"Look, Donald is Donald," says Southworth. "He was always like this. He was like that before and he's like that now. It's like there's a kid with a stick and an ant farm. He's the kid and we're the ant farm."

Finally, there was the tiny, lone-wolf entrepreneur named Andy Batkin.

In 2006, Batkin had the notion of a Million Dollar Golf Challenge. The idea was that 100 PGA Tour hopefuls—guys who hadn't yet made it—would put up $15,000 of their own cash for a chance to win $1 million.

Catchy hook, but Batkin needed a big name to give it sizzle, so he flew to Trump Tower to pitch The King of Deals. All Trump had to do, Batkin said, was add his glitzy name to it, do a few interviews, watch it all unfold in a one-hour special on ESPN, and he'd get a big flat fee.

"Just think," Batkin told Trump. "Someday, [NBC golf analyst] Johnny Miller might be saying, 'This guy got his start on Donald Trump's Million Dollar Challenge!' "

That excited Trump. "Really? Johnny Miller might say that?"

"Sure!"

Plus, Trump's people had an idea. If Batkin agreed to hold it at a Trump-branded golf course in the Caribbean, it would kill two birds with one stone. "Mr. Trump had to get down there anyway," says Ashley Cooper, who ran Trump's golf businesses at the time. "He owed them one trip down there [as part of a licensing deal] and he'd never seen the course. So it was a win-win on all sides."

Sold. Trump scrawled his seismometer autograph on the contract, and they were in business.

Fast forward…months later, to Trump's office, 10 minutes before the giant press conference to announce the big challenge. It was about to take place below in the giant, gilded lobby of Trump Tower.

Every local TV station in New York was there, plus over 50 photographers and reporters. Upstairs, Trump and Batkin waited to go down. The plan was that Trump would descend on his magnificent gold lobby escalator, wave, smile, get to the mic, and tell the world about the "incredible, really spectacular, amazing" million-dollar event that was coming to their lucky TV sets and how it would be "like nothing we've ever seen in golf."

Except as he sat in his office, Trump had a bomb sitting in his vest pocket, lit.

He turned to one of his underlings and said, "Tell me again why the fuck I'm doing this?"

Batkin's heart stopped for a second. What was this? With nine minutes to go?

The underling stammered a bit until Batkin interjected, "Well, because it's going to be great. And you get your fee, plus you have to go down there anyway."

"How much are you getting?" Trump barked.

Keep in mind, financially, Batkin was no *S.S. Trump.* He was a dinghy bobbing in the open sea. He'd taken out a $1.5 million personal loan to guarantee Trump the three-day event would come off. He desperately needed Trump and this press conference to beat the wannabe mini-tour golfers out of the bushes. The golfers would then pony up $15,000 to play for a chance at a cool million. "For a lot of them, they were going to have to borrow it from their uncles or their brothers," Batkin says. "But I didn't know if we'd really get guys to do it. I had everything I owned on the line."

With no Trump, he was a dead man.

Batkin tried to breathe.

If all went well, he told Trump, he was going to gross in the high six figures, but then he was going to have to start paying all kinds of people. A small bead of sweat trickled down his brow.

Trump chewed on that like it was an aspirin tablet.

"Fuck it," Trump said. "I'm not going down there until I get half."

Batkin just stared at him.

"I was glad I was wearing a dark suit," Batkin recalls. "Because I really thought I was about to soil it."

This is when Cooper, Trump's golf guy, tried to step in and douse the fire. "No, no, we're all right. Andy, tell him again your vision for this."

Batkin explained how this million-dollar challenge idea didn't have to stop at golf. It could be done with tennis, sailing, bowling, lots of things. "And you'd be in for all of it," he said to Trump.

That seemed to make Trump even madder. "Half," he said. "Otherwise, fuck it."

Batkin couldn't believe this was happening. He felt like he might puke. He checked his watch. Seven minutes. He swallowed hard and stared at the most famous business tycoon in the world.

"Donald, why should I change the deal?" Batkin said, firmly. "We have a signed contract."

Trump, in full scowl, stared at his shoes. Batkin felt like somebody had knitted sweaters for each of his teeth.

In TrumpWorld, this is the moment where the little guy knuckles under. Trump has the money, the lawyers, and the poker face to make you break. It always worked.

Except this time.

"Okay, fine," Batkin said. He got up to leave.

"Where are you going?" Trump said.

"Downstairs," Batkin said. "And when they ask me, 'Where's Donald?' I'm just going to say, 'Oh, five minutes ago, upstairs, he reneged on the deal. Tried to hold me up for half my company.' And then I'll take out these papers in my right hand and show them your signature."

Trump seethed but stayed put. Batkin got in the elevator. Trump's assistant, Carolyn Kepcher, ran into it with him.

"Andy, you can't do this! This is bad for everybody. Please don't do this!"

Batkin held up the papers and said, "Carolyn, we have a signed deal."

They descended, Carolyn trying to talk him out of it as they dropped. Batkin wasn't budging. This was a titanic risk he was taking. Why?

"Going into high school," Batkin recalls, "I was 4-foot-11. I knew all about bullies. My dad taught me how to box. He'd say, 'You get one good punch on their nose, that'll do it. You'll probably get way worse from them, but they won't come back.' And that's what I was thinking about. This guy is just another bully. I mean, it's Trump, so it was scary. But I knew I couldn't allow it, or I'd be sunk."

The elevator opened and they walked into the gilded Trump Tower lobby. Two minutes to go. It was almost time to start the press conference. Batkin was praying for a power blackout.

Finally, with 30 seconds left, he saw Trump's polished shoes coming down the escalator, like a god descending from Olympus. Trump was giving the packed lobby crowd his half-grin, waving at them, like nothing had happened.

Batkin finally inhaled again.

Trump came to the stage and shook Batkin's hand. They turned for pictures, all smiles. "I'd never seen that many flash-bulbs in my life," Batkin remembers.

Out of the side of his smile, Trump said, "You think anybody would be here without *me*?"

Batkin kept smiling and murmured back, "You think anybody would be here if you weren't holding my million-dollar check?"

11

TRUMP V. OBAMA

Obama ought to get off the golf course.
—DONALD J. TRUMP

I HAVE A BUDDY who has to hide his golf from his wife. She thinks he plays too much, which he probably does, so he can't post his scores. He can't talk about his round. He has to make up excuses for why he wasn't at his desk when she calls.

Trump has the same problem. Not with his wife. With the country. In his first 22 months as president, he played a documented 149 rounds, or about 1 every 4 days, according to TrumpGolfCount .com. He's taken so much heat about playing too much golf that he tries to hide it. Unlike my buddy, he's not very good at it.

For instance, one March, he said he was going to be working all day at Mar-a-Lago. But then Trump friend Chris Ruddy posted a picture of him shaking hands with somebody. On Trump's left hand was a golf glove.

Busted.

One summer day in 2018, as he was getting ready to leave for 10 days in Bedminster, he announced that he was going to be working and taking meetings the entire time. "This is not a golf trip!" The only problem was that when he left the White House, he was wearing a pair of FootJoy golf shoes.

What's strange is that, before he became president, he said he would do no such thing, ever, never. "I love golf," he told a crowd at a February 2016 campaign stop in Portsmouth, New Hampshire, "but if I were in the White House, I don't think I'd ever see Turnberry again. I don't think I'd ever see Doral again....I don't think I'd ever see many of the places that I have. I don't ever think I'd see anything—I just wanna stay in the White House and work my ass off, make great deals, right? Who's gonna leave?"

Who? Him. According to NBC News, in his first 579 days in office, he'd spent exactly one-third at one of his properties.

Trump threw gallons of shade at President Obama for allegedly neglecting his duties in favor of the golf course. He criticized him 27 times on Twitter alone for playing too much golf as president. Obama did play a lot of golf. In fact, halfway through his eighth year, Obama had played 250 rounds of golf in his presidency, a figure that astonished Trump. He nearly sprained his tweeting thumbs:

250 rounds...that's more golf than a guy on the PGA Tour plays!

Well, no. A PGA Tour player plays about 250 rounds per year. Over seven years, that would be 1,750 rounds, not 250. But get this: Over the 2018 Thanksgiving weekend, in Palm Beach, Trump played five straight days, more than anybody on the PGA Tour played that week.

Can you believe that, with all of the problems and difficulties facing the U.S., President Obama spent the day playing golf. Worse than Carter

Well, Carter didn't play golf. Obama also took one-third as many vacation days in his first year as Trump did in his (111). In fact, no modern president took as many vacation days in their first year as Trump. The only one to come close to Trump's vacation bonanza was Bush 43, who took about 70, mostly to his ranch in Texas, but in much bigger clumps, so the costs were far less.

We pay for Obama's travel so he can fundraise millions so Democrats can run on lies. Then we pay for his golf.

True, but some golf is more expensive than other golf. Obama played 61% of his rounds at nearby military courses like the one at Andrews Air Force Base, 35 minutes away from the White House. Trump never plays military or public courses. The only local course he plays is Trump Washington in Sterling, Virginia. Mostly, though, he prefers taking Air Force One down to Trump

International in West Palm Beach at a cost of $3.6 million per trip. To put that in perspective, Obama's yearly Martha's Vineyard vacations cost Americans $450,000, according to Judicial Watch.

Trump relished ripping Obama whenever he played on a big news day. When ISIS beheaded American photojournalist James Foley, Obama was playing in Martha's Vineyard. Trump even posted a video on Instagram of Obama smiling in a golf cart mixed with footage of the decapitation. In an ice-cold rebuke, he wrote:

Not under my watch.

When Trump became president, he'd see his golf clubs less than he'd see the White House basketball court. Who would have time? He'd be busy fixing the nation's problems, seven days a week. Except just the opposite happened. Trump is on a pace to play almost triple the amount of golf Obama played. Obama wound up playing 306 rounds in his 2,920 total days in office, or once every 9.5 days. Trump is on pace, over eight years, to obliterate Obama's number—at 759 rounds, which goes to show you that bone spurs do heal very nicely.

That 759 rounds would be third all-time, behind the record set by Woodrow Wilson's estimated 1,600 rounds and just a smidgen behind Eisenhower's estimated 800. Ike played so much golf, in fact, that a bumper sticker got popular: "BEN HOGAN

FOR PRESIDENT. IF WE'RE GOING TO HAVE A GOLFER, LET'S HAVE A GOOD ONE."

Anybody want to put Tiger Woods on a bumper sticker?

Much more importantly, to Trump critics, is that Trump's golf is exponentially more expensive. Through September 2018—19 months into his presidency—Trump's far-flung golf trips had cost American taxpayers an estimated $77 million. Just the Secret Service's cost of renting golf carts alone to protect him cost over $300,000, according to documents obtained by TMZ.

This might be why one American, Kathy Rentz, a Republican from Pennsylvania, scrawled across her IRS federal tax return, "Not for Trump's Golf Trips!"

It's not just the cost, it's the optics. On May 11, 2018, Trump's lawyer, Rudy Giuliani, declared that Trump was too busy to meet with FBI special investigator Robert Mueller. The next day, Trump played golf.

One February, Trump encouraged people to celebrate Martin Luther King Jr. Day with acts of kindness. "It's not a day to hang out in the park or pull out the barbecue grill," he said. "It's a day to do something to help someone else, and that can be as simple as...picking up the newspaper for that elderly person who can't get to the end of the driveway." Then he went out and played golf at Trump International. Maybe he was looking for newspapers?

In March of 2018, as 800,000 people were marching all over the country to protest the lack of gun control in America just after the Stoneman Douglas High School mass murders, he played golf.

Remember that round Trump played with pros Woods, Johnson, and Faxon in November of '17? As they made the turn that day, an aide took Trump aside and told him militants had just shot up and bombed an Egyptian mosque, an attack which would leave 311 dead. Wouldn't the president want to issue a statement immediately?

"I was in a golf cart with Trump," Faxon recalled to Medium .com. "I thought he'd have to go back to Mar-a-Lago and make a statement. There were hundreds of lives lost."

But Trump kept on playing. "The optics are going to look bad," Faxon remembered Trump telling the pro players. "I'm on a golf course and we have a disaster. The media will take this that I don't care, I'm gallivanting around with celebrity golfers. In reality, whether I'm in the White House, Mar-a-Lago, or on the golf course, my statement is not going to change."

FYI: Obama did *not* post a fake video on Instagram that day of Trump toodling along in a golf cart mixed with footage of bloody mosque murders.

But maybe the most tin-eared moment of his golfing annals was when he tweeted:

Heading to the Southern White House to watch the Funeral Service of Barbara Bush. First Lady Melania has arrived in Houston to pay our respects. Will be a beautiful day!

A day filled with grief and mourning? Let's play 36!
Sadly, he only got in 18.
What if Obama and Trump played *against each other*?
Please?
It's probably never going to happen, but for a time, Trump

wanted it to. "His swing looks like it's coming along beautiful," he once told the *New York Post*. "His game looks much better. I'd love to play him for the presidency." When Trump bought Virginia's Lowes Island golf course in 2009 and turned it into Trump Washington, D.C., he said he was hoping it would replace Congressional as the home course for Tiger Woods' annual PGA Tour event (it didn't) and that he was looking forward to playing it with President Obama. (He didn't.)

He could've. One time, in 2014, Obama was in Westchester and asked his staff to set up a game at Trump Westchester. It's unclear what happened, but some say Trump wouldn't allow it because it meant closing down his course for his members for part of the day. He did, however, club Obama over the head with a tweet:

> **If Obama resigns from office NOW, thereby doing a great service to the country—I will give him free lifetime golf at any one of my courses!**

Let's say there is a god for golf writers and it's on—Obama v. Trump—18 holes, loser has to wash the other's limo in a Speedo. Who would win?

Wait! Before you lay down your bets, let's consider...

*Cheating...

If Trump is playing, he's cheating. Apart from conceding short gimmes, Obama does not cheat. Trump always shoots in the

70s whether he did or not. He's 80 proof. For The Donald, golf is never about improving or the exercise or enjoying the day. It's about beating you, no matter what it takes to do it. Obama plays like he sleeps with the USGA rule book under his pillow. He's a stickler. Everything is by the book.

"I can definitely vouch for #44 in his integrity on the course," emails basketball star Stephen Curry of the Golden State Warriors. "The man knows how to enjoy the game and do it the right way for sure. Except we only played for $1 so the stakes weren't that high."

Wait. No mulligans, no my foot slipped's, no gimme chip-ins?

"No," Curry writes.

So if we're playing this match with five USGA rules officials following each president with cameras, then Trump won't be able to cheat, which means he'll be out of his element, doing something new, and that's never good in a pressure match.

Advantage: Obama.

*Putting…

Trump picks up every putt within six feet and, if you're not a threat, will pick up yours, too. You could park an Airstream trailer in Trump's Friendship Zone. He gives so many putts, it gets a little emasculating. "A month or so ago I gave a guy a 10-footer," Trump told *Golf* magazine in 2010, "and it was more insulting giving it to him then *not* giving it to him. You don't want him to think you feel sorry for him. It's a very fine line."

You heard that right. Trump *gives* 10-foot putts. If this were basketball, it'd be the equivalent of saying, "Don't even bother taking that 3. You'll never miss that."

Still, Trump is an excellent putter. Obama not so much.

Advantage: Trump.

*Handicaps...

Obama came into office as a 17 handicap and left as about a 13—"an honest 13," he says. The ESPN sportscaster Michael Wilbon, a frequent partner of Obama's on the course, estimates him to be an 11 now. Trump's 2.8 is a bigger lie than Clinton's "I did not have sex with that woman," but he brags about it so he'd be stuck giving Obama eight shots. That means on the eight hardest holes, Obama could take one shot off his true score for purposes of the bet. To win any of those eight holes, Trump would have to beat him by two shots.

Giant advantage: Obama.

But let's say they played straight up, with no shots given.

Advantage: Trump.

So who would win?

"I would win," Trump said at a rally in Bluffton, South Carolina, once. "No, seriously, I would."

If they had to walk? Obama by 20.

But let's say they get to arguing. Let's say Obama catches Trump cheating and fronts him, and Trump throws his phantom Winged Foot punch again. Who wins the fight?

Well, they're about the same height, no matter what the White House doctor says, but Trump outweighs Obama by a good 75 pounds. Obama, though, is 15 years younger, is light years faster, and works out constantly. Trump's idea of exercise is, as he told the *New York Times*, standing in front of a podium for an hour. "That's exercise," he says.

Advantage: Obama.

Plus, Obama is left-handed, so if he could slip that first Trump haymaker, he could surprise the big ginger with a hard left and maybe knock him out cold.

At which point, Obama could lean over him and say, "Not on my watch."

PROFESSIONAL PEST

He's not as smart as we thought he was.

—ARNOLD PALMER

THE WORLD OF PROFESSIONAL golf is just slightly more Republican than a Cabela's grand opening. In a poll done by Golf.com, players were asked if the USGA and PGA should move their tournaments off of Trump's courses as a reaction to his incendiary comments about Mexicans and immigrants. A fat 88% said no. Only 4% said yes. A full 42% of them said they'd vote for him again, compared to 20% who wouldn't. The Philadelphia Eagles and the Golden State Warriors might refuse to come to the White House, but 90% of Tour players would be on the first NetJet there.

Caddies? Not so much.

In October of 2017, at Liberty National Golf Club in Jersey City, New Jersey, Trump became the first standing president to attend the President's Cup, a Ryder-Cup-wannabe event that pits the 12 best American players against the world's 12 best players not from Europe, if that makes any sense. It's that age-old America versus Australia-South Africa-Fiji-Asia-Latin America-And-A-Few-Others battle. That year, America swamped the ASAFALAAAFOs, 19–11. When it was time for the trophy presentation, Trump and his massive entourage of Secret Service, SWAT guys, press ops, and assistants were all flowing out of his luxury box to the 18th green, when swimming against the tide was a caddy of one of the winning American players. He was stopped cold by two agents, who put big hands on each of his shoulders.

"Sir, where are you going?"

"I'm just walking," the caddy said. "Can't I walk?"

"Sir, you're the only one going this direction. Where are you going?"

Their grips got tighter. They weren't blinking.

The caddy looked at both of them and sighed. "Look, guys, I appreciate you have a job to do and I mean no disrespect, but I just can't stand to be anywhere near that motherfucker you work for."

The agents loosed tiny smiles and let him go. A few minutes later, Trump gathered with the best golfers on the planet, raised the trophy high, and dedicated it to a very surprising group of people.

"On behalf of all the people of Texas, and all of the people of...Puerto Rico and the people of Florida, that have really suffered over this last short period of time with the hurricanes, I want to just remember them and we're going to dedicate this trophy to all of those people who went through so much."

It was a bizarre choice. At that moment, Puerto Rico was begging for U.S. help to restore electricity and water and not getting much. The entire $300 million contract to get the electricity turned back on had been handed to a tiny company out of Whitefish, Montana, the hometown of Trump's then Interior Secretary Ryan Zinke, whose son worked for a time for the company. With thousands of people trapped in their homes without power or water—filling out a grisly death toll that would eventually rise to 3,000 people—a golf trophy didn't seem all that helpful.

Just then, a fan hollered out: "You don't give a sh*t about Puerto Rico!"

Golf takes long hours, piles of money, and manicured acres to play, so it mostly leans toward the rich, except when it leans to the very rich. The people who watch it on TV are the toniest demographic of any sport, which is why the products being pitched are usually luxury cars, Wall Street companies, and watches that cost more than some people's houses. Those corporate boards lean politically the same way as the players, but they need rich Democrat fans to buy, too, so Trump has been an uncaged lion for them.

Take, for instance, Cadillac.

Cadillac's Trump problems began with an idle promise Trump made to the Palm Beach County commissioners long before he was president, back when he was trying to get the land near

Mar-a-Lago to build Trump International (West Palm Beach). He told them, "If you lease me the land, I promise you I'll get you a Tour stop." The commissioner of the PGA Tour then was an achingly quiet guy named Tim Finchem, who would rather administer gallbladder surgery on himself than rock the corporate boat. He knew Trump could rock a cruise liner, and he wanted no part of him as a business partner. So Trump wasn't getting any Tour stop. No way. That idea was dead. Still, when Trump gets his heart set on something, he will turn oceans into deserts to get it. He wanted a Tour stop no matter what, which meant there was only one other way—buy a course that already HAD a Tour stop.

Enter Doral.

Since 1962, Doral's Blue Monster course in Miami had been a classic stop on the PGA Tour's Florida swing, a straw-hat old-school tourney won by no less than Jack Nicklaus and Nick Faldo. Only the Masters, Pebble Beach, and the Colonial had been Tour stops longer than Doral. So, in 2012, Trump bought the entire Doral resort out of bankruptcy for $150 million—lock, stock, and all four courses, plus the hotel, by far his largest golf purchase ever. He changed the signs immediately, calling it Trump National Doral Miami. He declared Doral's Tour stop "a major," which it most assuredly wasn't, and told the press he now had "the greatest site in Florida," which he absolutely didn't. Still, Trump had his wish. Finchem and the PGA Tour would now be coming to *him*, at *his* course, and *he* could take center stage for one week as the New God of Golf. That's when the trouble started.

The sponsor of the Doral stop was Cadillac, and suddenly,

Cadillac was having to share top billing with Trump and his King Kong personality and his shooting-gallery press conferences and his helicopter flying in from West Palm with the giant TRUMP painted on its side, the TV cameras lapping it up. There is only one star at any Trump event and it's the Donald.

"Trump was getting more commercial air time than Cadillac," said a person involved in the sponsorship. "He parked his damn helicopter in the middle of the golf course. Here was Cadillac, paying all that money, and the whole tournament was suddenly all about Trump." Said another, "They were getting dwarfed. No way were they going to get their money's worth with Trump there."

Trump loved the attention, driving his supercharged cart up behind golfers (a no-no), interrupting players during practice rounds (not cool), and being sure to be seen whenever and wherever possible (as you'd expect).

"You should've seen him," says one caddy of an American player. "He'd come out to the (practice) range and go down the line with the same script for each guy. He'd come up to the first guy and go, 'Hey, you're lookin' really good!' Then he'd point to the guy hitting balls next to him and go, "But I don't know if you can beat THIS guy!' So then he'd go to that guy and say, 'Hey, you're looking really good! But I don't think you can beat THIS guy' and so on. Made me wanna hurl."

Cadillac asked Trump if he could please tone it down and stop flying his chopper in during the tournament. "Maybe you could fly in before play starts?" they asked. He owned the hotel; could he maybe just stay put at Doral for the four days? Trump said he'd consider it, but he kept choppering in during play, a killer cutaway shot for any TV director. *Here comes The Man himself!*

Worse, the players were starting to grumble about the course. Not long after he bought it, Trump had architect Gil Hanse re-do the Blue Monster. Hanse, with Trump by his side at every step, somehow gave Doral a charm bypass. He added length and difficulty but took out the character. Doral became nothing but a Big Bangers Ball—only long hitters invited. A tournament that had been won by smaller, crafty players like Lee Trevino, Tom Kite, and Ben Crenshaw was now only winnable by the beasts, like Tiger Woods and Dustin Johnson (twice). Cue the grousing and grumbling in the locker room. After he finished that first week, a reporter asked four-time major winner Rory McIlroy what his takeaway was on the new Doral.

"My takeaway?" McIlroy said. "Maybe it's time for me to reconsider my schedule."

"They made it too long," says architect Bobby Jones. "Dick Wilson [the original designer] had already made a terrific course, a tough course, but you know Gil [Hanse] was gonna do whatever Donald said." Says that caddy, "Doral is a disaster now. Way too long. It's just a slog now. Only 15 guys can win it—the 15 longest guys."

That, of course, delighted Trump. He loved seeing the best players in the world shoot 78s on his Monster. It was somehow a reflection on his own golf skill. "He's one of a kind," Tour star Rickie Fowler said of Trump with a laugh. "He likes seeing us get beat up by his golf course."

It all became too much for Cadillac. They bailed out. Two months before the election, the Tour moved the tournament from Doral to Mexico. After 55 years at Doral, Trump's ached-for Tour stop up and emigrated to Mexico on him. "It's quite ironic that we're going to Mexico after being at Doral," McIlroy said with a grin. "We just jump over the wall."

Today, Doral isn't half the place it used to be. I visited it in May of 2018 and found it . . . empty. "Doral is a conference resort," said the now-late general manager of The Breakers hotel, David Burke. "Big groups, corporate events. But Trump is so controversial now, corporations don't want to risk pissing their clients off by staying at a property with 'Trump' in the title. My buddy runs it and he says they're empty."

Forbes confirms this. They report that Doral lost 100,000 booked room nights since Trump took over the White House. Worse, *Forbes* reports that revenue at Trump's U.S. golf properties fell by an estimated 9% in 2017. When Trump broke tradition with every modern president and refused to sell his businesses or at least put them in a blind trust, he must've figured he'd make much more money his way. Turned out just the opposite. Most financial experts say if he'd have sold it all and put everything into America's bull market, he'd be worth $500 million more today.

When I visited Doral in May of 2018, it was like somebody had pulled a fire alarm. I stood outside the pro shop at a spot where I could see half a dozen golf holes but only saw one (1) golf cart. The practice range had room for 50 people, but only two were there. There was one kid taking a tennis lesson. There were the standard 100-foot poles waving flags the size of a Chili's, miles of marble and gold and plush carpet, the standard belching Venetian fountain, just nobody gawking at them. It was so empty that an oddly serendipitous thing happened. Twelve hours after I checked out in the main lobby, a gunman entered that lobby, draped a massive American flag over the front desk, started screaming that he wanted to see Trump, and began shooting the joint up with a machine gun. He shot everywhere—shattering the gilded mirrors, the massive chandeliers, and the huge windows. He was eventually shot in the leg by Miami police and apprehended. But here's the good thing: The place was so empty nobody got hit. Zero deaths, zero injuries.

It was the rarest event for Trump: A loss even he couldn't spin into a win. Though he did come up with a pretty good line. "I hope they have kidnapping insurance," Trump said.

So the next time you hear somebody say, "Name one good thing Trump has ever done for people," you can point out that he saved a lot of lives that day.

(A note from our Irony Dept.: Trump Doral has managed to sign a pro tour golf event again, but it's on the PGA's Latin American Tour. Hope they have machine-gun insurance.)

Dumping the Doral Tour stop wasn't the first time pro golf ran from Trump. For 36 years, there existed a silly-season event called the PGA Grand Slam. It was a fabricated event, usually played in exotic places, pitting the winners of the four majors against each other, for no apparent reason. In 2015, it was supposed to move to Trump Los Angeles in Rancho Palos Verdes,

California. But then Trump opened up his presidential campaign by declaring that Mexican immigrants to the U.S. were "bringing drugs. They're bringing crime. They're rapists. And some, I assume, are good people."

Golf buried its head and groaned, but Trump didn't apologize. Double Down doubled down. He told the Golf Channel he'd received "tremendous support" from the golf world because "they all know I'm right."

That was too much. The PGA Tour, LPGA Tour, USGA, and PGA of America rose up to yell, "It's not true." They issued this statement:

> In response to Mr. Trump's comments about the golf industry "knowing he is right" in regards to his recent statements about Mexican immigrants, we feel compelled to clarify that those remarks do not reflect the views of our organizations....Mr. Trump's comments are inconsistent with our strong commitment to an inclusive and welcoming environment in the game of golf.

It's a triple blue moon when the stodgy world of golf takes a stance on anything political, but this time, it was pissed enough to not just speak but act. The PGA of America refused to play the Grand Slam at Trump's course and then canceled the Grand Slam altogether. It hasn't come back since. What do you know about that? A golf-crazy presidential candidate killed two pro golf tournaments in two years.

It hurts Trump deeply when pro golf rejects him this way.

He knows pro golf like a blind man knows his room. He knows who's who, even down to the golf writers.

Once, during the presidential campaign, a pro from Trump Bedminster, Jim Herman, won the 2016 Houston Open. Trump had staked him on Tour to help him get his start, and Herman's win was a huge surprise. Steve DiMeglio, the longtime golf writer from *USA Today*, called the campaign in hopes they could fetch him one quote from Trump about Herman. It was a long shot. Trump was stumping in Milwaukee, where it was madness. Every political writer was dying for time with the primary-gobbling phenomenon.

All of a sudden, DiMeglio was on the phone with Trump, who was going on and on about Herman, what a great guy he is, what a great player, "I always believed in him," and "We're so proud," etc., nonstop. Finally, in the background, DiMeglio heard, "Can somebody get him the fuck off the phone? He's supposed to be on stage! Who's he talking to anyway?" Then DiMeglio heard, "Some golf writer from *USA Today*."

"I heard about that from our political writers for a while afterward," DiMeglio remembers with a laugh. " 'How the *hell* did you get Trump again?' "

Now that he's president, Trump can get some of America's most famous team-sport pro athletes to play with him. According to TrumpGolfCount.com, he has a pro athlete in his foursome 45% of the time. And why not? Trump is a good player, and athletes are usually good, too, which allows the whole parade to fly along in under three and a half hours, the way he likes it. Among the dozens of athletes he's played with are Peyton Manning, Tom Brady, Kirk Cousins, and John Elway.

He's always been able to get games with the most famous golfers in the world: Jack Nicklaus, Arnold Palmer, Gary Player, and Greg Norman. As president, that hasn't changed. So far, he's teed it up with Tiger Woods, Rory McIlroy, Dustin Johnson (twice), Rickie Fowler, and more. Bryson DeChambeau gave him a golf bag. Trump's most frequent pro partner since he's been president has been David Frost (four times), not the deceased talk-show host but the journeyman South African.

They all say the same thing: He's great fun and they have no idea what he shot. Only Rory McIlroy guessed at it. "He probably shot around 80. He's a decent player for a guy in his 70s.... Sometimes he will give himself some putts, but that's fine, he's the president, he can have that luxury."

Woods: "Our discussion topics were wide-ranging; it was fun. We both enjoyed the bantering, bickering, and needling.... We didn't have a match and played for fun." (This, of course, turned out to be a fib, as innocently revealed by Brad Faxon to me in Chapter 4.)

Justin Thomas: "I've never seen that many golf carts on one hole in my life."

Japanese star Hideki Matsuyama got to play one day not only with Trump but also with Japanese prime minister Shinzō Abe. Through an interpreter, he said: "I had no idea what it would be like, only what I'd read in the media, but he wasn't like they say he is at all. He was fun. It was enjoyable. We chatted the whole day. He asked me so many questions. About Japan. About how I like America. He offered me whatever help I needed. I was really nervous, but at least my first drive went straight."

Did either leader cheat?

"Well, we weren't betting. There was nothing riding on it. They weren't professional golfers. They were just trying to have fun, so it was a very easy and enjoyable day."

(In other words: *Hai.*)

Jack Nicklaus likes Trump and stands up for him against critics, but then again, Trump has given him good work at his golf courses, especially Trump Ferry Point in the Bronx.

Trump used to like to tell people he was tight with the late, great Arnold Palmer, too. Once, the golf writer James Dodson was leaving an interview with Trump to go to one with Palmer. Dodson says Trump "crossed one finger over the other and he said, 'Arnold and I are like that.'" Dodson remembered, "And I told Arnold that the next night at dinner, and he laughed and said, 'Really? It's more like this.' And he crossed his hands and put them at his own throat."

"One moment stands out in my mind," Palmer's daughter, Peg, recounted recently to writer Thomas Hauser of the *Sporting News*. "My dad and I were at home in Latrobe. He died in September [2016], so this was before the election. The television was on. Trump was talking. And my dad made a sound of disgust—like 'uck' or 'ugg'—like he couldn't believe the arrogance and crudeness of this man who was the nominee of the political party that he believed in. Then he said, 'He's not as smart as we thought he was,' and walked out of the room. What would my dad think of Donald Trump today? I think he'd cringe."

Trump often calls Tiger his "good friend," but it seems to be a one-way friendship. Woods did design Trump World Dubai, though it's not owned by Trump, only operated by him. Still, Eric Trump—who seems to have gone to the Donald Trump School of Fabulousness—thinks it's just another sign that they're super bros. "They've been very, very close," Eric said. "When you combine Trump and Tiger, it's a match made in heaven. It's a very amazing combination."

Yet every time we ask Tiger about Trump, it's like we asked him about an uncle who's in Leavenworth. "Well, he's the president of the United States. You have to respect the office. No matter who is in the office, you may like, dislike personality or the politics, but we all must respect the office." If that's true, then why did Woods' spokesman Glenn Greenspan try to build an O'Hare runway between the two of them? "Tiger is not in partnership with Mr. Trump or his organization and stating otherwise is absolutely wrong. Tiger Woods Design's contract and obligation is to the developer, DAMAC Properties. Our association ends there. I can't put it any clearer that Tiger Woods Design does *not* have an agreement with Mr. Trump."

When Trump eliminated protection for the 800,000 DACA "Dreamers," putting American-born young people at risk of being deported to countries they'd never even seen, Woods was in a pickle. The Tiger Woods Foundation is very involved in funding the educations of underprivileged kids from immigrant families. This was everything they didn't believe in. Its own foundation kids were terrified. The Tiger Woods Foundation had to tweet out:

We are committed to and in full support of our #DACA scholars and alumni. Join us in urging Congress to pass the #DREAMAct. #DefendDREAMers.

All doubt was removed the night Tiger went on *The Late Show with Stephen Colbert*, where Colbert asked him about the presidents with whom he'd played. Tiger recalled Bush 41 ("We played in about two hours"), Clinton ("lotsa cuts," which is to say, "sliced shots"), and Obama ("very competitive").

"What about Trump?" Colbert asked.

Woods got a big grin on his face and replied, "You said 'presidents,'" getting a big laugh from the crowd.

Trump does seem to be friends with Dustin Johnson, who lives in Palm Beach Gardens—20 minutes from Mar-a-Lago—and his grandfather, Art Whisnant (who was once drafted by the Minneapolis Lakers) lives in West Palm Beach. Trump once asked Johnson to come have Thanksgiving dinner with him, according to Whisnant. "They're tight," the grandfather says. So tight that on Tuesday of the 2018 U.S. Open week at Shinnecock Hills, New York, Johnson drove clear back into the city to appear at the opening of Trump's new clubhouse at Trump Ferry Point in the Bronx. Tiger wouldn't do a Tuesday appearance on Open week if you gave him Queens.

But playing golf with Trump can cause some serious blowback. Take what happened to McIlroy. He got pilloried for it.

"History will brutally judge [McIlroy's] golfing buddy Trump," wrote Ewan MacKenna in *The Irish Independent*. "But we ought to judge Rory right now."

McIlroy was so rattled by the reaction, he jumped on Twitter and vented.

I don't agree with everything my friends or family say or do, but I still play golf with them. To be called a fascist and a bigot by some people because I spent time in someone's company is just ridiculous. I hope, to some degree, this clarifies my decision to accept the invitation.

He also said he'd "think twice" about doing it again.

Trump really is tight with the one and only Long John Daly, who calls him his "great friend" and who came to the White House three months into Trump's reign with no less than Sarah Palin, Kid Rock, and ultra-right-wing rocker Ted Nugent. There, the foursome gleefully posed for a mocking photo in front of a painting of Hillary Clinton. Seems right that Daly would be one of the first celebrities Trump invited. Between them, Trump and Daly have fathered eight children and married seven different women.

Then there was the night a gaggle of Tour players and officials visited the White House. Among the Tour players were DeChambeau, Jason Bohn, Kevin Streelman, and Billy Hurley. Tour commissioner Jay Monahan was there, too.

"We walk into the Oval Office about 8 p.m. and there he is at the desk, still in his suit," Streelman recalls. "He jumps up and goes, 'My golf guys!' He seemed happy to see us and he couldn't have been more friendly. He let us take pictures, showed us around, and then he goes, 'You guys want to see the Lincoln Bedroom?' Next thing you know we're in the Lincoln Bedroom.... Then he says, 'Come with me.' We're in the Private Residence! He knocks on this one door, pretty loud, and goes, 'Melania? Are you decent? I got some guys I want you to meet.' After a while, she came out and we got to meet her, too! I mean, it was awesome! It was like we were his golf buddies and he was just showing us around his house! Just like a normal guy!"

(Trump also has a fun little trick he likes to play with visitors. He'll show people a button under his desk. It looks important. "You want me to push it?" he'll say. Before they can holler, "No!!!" he hits it. Instantly, a butler brings him another Diet Coke.)

Trump also calls Tour superstar Phil Mickelson "a good friend." They've played a couple times together, plus Mickelson is scheduled to design a Trump-operated course in Bali. But since the election, Mickelson has gone stone-cold mum on the subject. When I asked Mickelson about his friendship with Trump, he looked me right in the eye for about 10 seconds, smiled, and walked away.

Then there's Bernhard Langer, the sensational German who's dominated the Senior Tour. Trump says Langer is a "friend" and even offered a story about Langer to defend his own outrageous lie that "3 to 5 million people voted illegally" to help Hillary Clinton win the popular vote tally. Trump declared that Langer, a Florida resident, had been unable to vote at his usual polling place while several people "who did not look as if they should be allowed to vote" were ushered through.

It's a lovely story except for one small fact: Langer is a German citizen. He can't vote here.

One of Trump's goals when he got into the golf business was to someday see a golf major played on one of his courses. Since the Masters is permanently held at Augusta National (GA), that left him three options: the U.S. Open, the Open Championship (formerly the British Open), and the PGA Championship. It took him about 20 years, but the dream is about to become real. In 2022, the 104th PGA Championship will be held at Trump Bedminster.

The PGA announced the selection years before even Trump himself thought he'd ever be president. When Trump started running and began insulting everybody from Muslims to McCain, the PGA czars started getting nauseous. "What could we do?" says one PGA official. "We had a signed contract. We couldn't back out." If Trump is re-elected in 2020, that PGA would be in the middle of his fifth year.

A U.S. Open, though, might be out of the question. Even Trump admits that if he really wants a U.S. Open he's going to have to take his name off Trump Bedminster, which is his best chance to land one. "But my courses are all booming," he explained. "Without the name, they don't boom." Which is an odd thing to hear from a man who has declared that all his courses are the greatest layouts on the best pieces of property with the best members in the world. Why would they need the name?

U.S. Open sites are set through 2027, and none of them are

at Trump properties. Eight of those next nine will be in states where Trump has courses, and most of them will be played on tracks that he's said are inferior to his, including two at the "highly overrated" Pebble Beach.

Nobody better buy a damn shirt.

As to a Trump overseas course hosting an Open Championship in Europe, it's remotely possible, just not anytime soon. His course in Aberdeen is getting passed over left and right. Word was it would host three years of Scottish Opens beginning in 2019, but now the Scottish Open will go to a rival course two hours away, The Renaissance Club, designed by American Tom Doak. If it weren't for his name on it, Trump Turnberry would absolutely get the Open Championship. Since Trump bought the course, he's improved it so much it'd be a joke not to have one there. But the R&A has announced its Open schedule through 2022, with no Trump Turnberry in sight.

"He'll never get an Open Championship as long as he's the president," says John Huggan, the Scottish golf writer. "And, for sure, not as long as his name is on the course." Huggan says it's a bad match: Trump plus the walking dandruff balls that run the Royal and Ancient, the governing body that runs the Open. "All those R&A stiffs—'Oh, jolly good,' 'More tea?', and all that—and here comes this extroverted blowhard. No way. They'd never do it."

Would it help if he dedicated a trophy to them?

13

E W W W W W

It doesn't really matter what [they] write as long as you've
got a young and beautiful piece of ass.
—DONALD J. TRUMP

AMONG THE INVITED AT the opening of Trump Bedminster in
2004 was the former owner of the estate, bankrupt car legend
John DeLorean, then 79. Trump was standing with a gaggle of
golf writers when DeLorean drove up in a golf cart with his girlfriend in tow.

"Trump introduced them to everybody," remembers Eamon
Lynch, a columnist and Golf Channel personality. "He and
Trump visited for a while. Then DeLorean left. Trump turned to
us and said, 'The poor guy. He's a very old, sad figure. He's lost all
his money. And worst of all, his girlfriend is a solid 4.'"

Trump looks at women the same way he looks at golf trophies.

They're fun to collect and it's okay to cheat to get them. When he introduced me to Melania the first time, he said, "Look at her."

"What do you mean?"

"Look at her!"

"I just did look at her."

"No, look at her! Up and down. It's okay."

"Donald, I'm *not* going to look at her like that."

"Look at her! She likes it!"

So, red-faced, I quickly looked down at her shoes and back up in 1/10th of a second. He was grinning.

"All real."

As his women employees at Trump Los Angeles found out, he's not particularly interested in women for their SAT scores. This is how he's always been. Even at military school, he was called "ladies' man." The idea that women are individual human beings with brains and goals and ideas doesn't register much under the big orange canopy. At Trump Turnberry, it came out that the men get more than twice the bonus the women get, according to *The Scotsman*.

The most important quality in a Trump wife is that she be a 10 who doesn't play golf, doesn't care much about business, and doesn't watch too carefully. At that same Bedminster opening where Trump was holding court with that same gaggle of writers, a man in a suit came up with news. "Guess what? The Trump family has been selected Golf Family of the Year!"

Lynch remembers Trump thanking the guy, who then drove off. "Then Trump turns and says to us, 'Well, that tells me I can't get caught having an affair for the next year.'"

That's not easy. To Trump, women are like French fries. He knows he should stay away from them, but he can't keep his hands off. That can cause trouble for a man as famous as he is. A TV producer who spent time around him remembers Trump's infamous security guy, Keith Schiller, standing behind them during certain shoots. "He'd say, 'Don't shoot the redhead' or 'Stay off the blonde.' So I'm trying to frame the shots in these weird ways to keep these women out of the shot. It was nuts."

Someday, at the Smithsonian Museum, they should have an exhibit on the 2006 weekend Trump spent at the American Century Celebrity Challenge in Lake Tahoe, California, perhaps with a vat of Purell for afterward.

Despite the fact that he'd just turned 60, Trump, who was married at the time, not only played three full days of golf, he managed to bed a porn star, sleep with a Playmate of the Year, and grope a second porn star, as alleged by her two female friends. You talk about stamina.

NBC's golfapalooza, held at the Edgewood Tahoe resort in Lake Tahoe, is a boozy soup of golf and groupies and celebrities, many of them A-list pro athletes. That July, Aaron Rodgers, Drew Brees, and Ben Roethlisberger played. They also sprinkled in a few golfing nonathlete celebs, like actor Anthony Anderson, broadcaster Al Michaels, and comedian Ray Romano. Trump, with a hot NBC show called *The Apprentice* in its second year, was as sought after as any of them.

The presence of all those celebrities is why so many eligible women end up congregating for the wild nights at the official tournament hotel, Harrah's Casino. It's a *Guys Gone Wild* kind of weekend. Adult-film studio porn-house Wicked Pictures even had a booth in the gifting room to hype its latest, uh, releases. It stocked the room with swag and stars, including two of its leading ladies: Stephanie Clifford, aka "Stormy Daniels," and Jessica Drake. Cleavage and lipstick ready, the XXX stars lured plenty of male celebs in, including a certain amorous real estate owner in a red hat named Donald J. Trump, who'd seen Daniels earlier that day on the golf course. He came in and got a very famous photo with her, much to his regret 11 years later.

But it didn't stop at the photo. They got to talking, flirting, dining, and, finally, according to Daniels, having sex that night in Trump's suite.

Judging just on virility, you'd have to agree a 60-year-old man bedding a famous porn star is something of an achievement. But it wasn't good enough for Trump. He apparently went for seconds. According to Jessica Drake, Trump came *back* the next morning to the Wicked booth and began flirting with her, too. He invited her to walk with him during his round that day, which she did. He got her number and invited her up to his suite that night. That made her a little queasy. She'd heard stories from Daniels about Trump "chasing her" around his room "in his tighty-whities." So she brought two female friends as backup.

"When we entered the room," Drake recalled at a Gloria Allred–run press conference, "he grabbed each of us tightly in a hug and kissed each one of us without asking permission. He was wearing pajamas." Trump asked them a lot of questions about life as a porn star, and then they left "30 or 45 minutes later," Drake said. She says Trump called her later and offered her $10,000 for sex. As a form of seduction, Drake wasn't impressed. In fact, she said it wasn't "acceptable behavior for anyone, much less a presidential candidate" and tagged him a "sexual assault apologist."

Even two porn stars didn't do the trick. Somewhere in the middle of all that, Trump allegedly fit in a bedding of Playmate Karen McDougal, whom he'd been having an affair with and had flown in for the occasion. How's that for depth of douchery? When you're cheating on the mistress with whom you're cheating on your wife, you've entered a kind of infidelity *Inception*.

And where was his new bride of six months, Melania, during these Mattress Olympics? Back in New York with their new four-month-old baby, Barron.

This wasn't the first time Trump cheated at a golf tournament. He cheated on his then-girlfriend soon-to-be wife Marla Maples at the 1993 AT&T Pebble Beach Pro-Am, according to *San Francisco Chronicle* society columnist Pat Steger. She wrote in her column:

> Donald Trump had a great time at…Pebble Beach, but not such a great time was had by Marla Maples who joined him mid-tournament—which meant that the gorgeous blond model he brought with him, who does Frederick's of Hollywood catalogs, had to go home to L.A.

Stranger still, Maples had flown in with a wedding dress in her suitcase, expecting to marry Trump that Saturday afternoon, but Trump 86'd it at the last minute, Steger wrote. True to form, Maples was pregnant with daughter Tiffany at the time.

And now let's all break for a shower.

* * *

The irony is Trump has been one of the best friends the Ladies Professional Golf Association (LPGA) Tour ever had. He knows the players, knows the tournaments, and loves being involved. And, yes, it's probably just coincidence that his favorite LPGA star is also one of its most photogenic players, its blond bombshell, Natalie Gulbis.

Gulbis, a four-time tournament winner, first met Trump at the LPGA's season-ending ADT Championship, at Trump International in West Palm Beach, Florida. The ADT was as fancy as it got in the LPGA, a crescendo that featured only the Tour's 30 best players. It even allowed Trump to show off Mar-a-Lago— where the players and top officials stayed. Trump relished the idea of 30 female golf pros at his disposal. He'd come down every morning of the tournament and weave through the omelettes.

"Natalie!" he roared one morning in 2005. "Congratulations on making it to your first Tour championship. I see you're leading the tour in birdies this year. What do you think of the course?"

Gulbis was amazed. "How did he even *know* that?" She loved how he seemed to care about her, asking so many questions, inquiring about her love life, advising her on agents and corporate sponsor and moves to make in her career.

"He believed any notion that I should accept less money than a PGA Tour player for appearances or endorsement contracts was just plain wrong," she told a reporter. He even tried to help her love life. At the time, Gulbis was dating the aforementioned Roethlisberger, the 6-foot-5 Pittsburgh Steelers quarterback, but he'd eventually break it off with her, leaving Gulbis publicly heartbroken. Trump told more than one friend that Roethlisberger broke up with her because she had "no tits," according to golf writer Kevin Cook. What was Trump's love advice to Gulbis? Lie. "From now on I want to read that you dumped him," he insisted.

Trump was lavishly generous at the ADT, and the players loved it. But it wasn't long before they experienced some Trump trickery. In fact, it was the first year, 2001. The players had torn it up in Round 1 with some low scores. Trump wasn't having that. A Trump course is not a welcome mat. He sent his crew out that evening to shave lake banks and speed the greens up to faster than the hood of a Buick, and had them stop cutting the rough, according to players. As a result, nearly every player in the field scored worse from Round 1 to Round 2, which is unheard of in pro golf unless there's suddenly bad weather, which there wasn't. The winner, Hall of Famer Karrie Webb, was six shots worse that second day. The redoubtable Annika Sörenstam, who finished second, was also six worse. Major-winner Grace Park was nine.

The Trumpster was delighted. He kept driving around in his turbo cart, asking players, "How about this course, huh? Tough, huh? When's the last time you shot this high?"

"When I was nine," one said.

"He definitely instructed his staff to change the preparation of the golf course," says LPGA Hall of Famer Dottie Pepper, now an on-course reporter for NBC. "How do you prepare for one course on Thursday and then have to play a completely different course Friday? The players were ticked off. But there was nothing we could do. And the LPGA wouldn't stand up to him. They'd just say, 'It's Donald Trump. We're lucky to have him.'"

But were they? Letting Donald Trump host a women's golf tournament is like letting Justin Bieber babysit. There's bound to be trouble. For one thing, Trump would kick off the pro-am by having his 727 buzz the course, causing panic in Palm Beach. The West Palm Beach airport switchboard would light up with people sure a plane was crashing. "People would be freaking out," says one airport official. "Are we getting bombed?'"

"Everything he does to the country now, as president, he did to us beforehand, in golf," says a then-high-ranking LPGA official who doesn't particularly want the most powerful man in the world knowing who she is. "Like, he sent us this astronomical bill for the media hospitality. He charged us for more media than you could've possibly crammed in that room. There weren't even that many there to begin with, but he charged us for way, way more that weren't there. And he kept unloading merchandise he didn't want from his pro shop right out in front.

"One of my closest friends came and brought a group of people to see the tournament. So I said, great, let's all have dinner at Mar-a-Lago. We sat behind a big door, totally hidden, so Donald wouldn't bother us. After a while, I looked up and saw him coming in. I'm like, 'Uh-oh.' He sees us, pulls up a chair, without even asking, takes off his jacket and says, 'Well now I know why Oprah is such a big fat slob.' Well, my friend is from the south. She's *very* proper. I thought she was going to swallow her fork. Why was he bringing up Oprah around us? We weren't even talking about Oprah. 'You know, she was here last weekend; she couldn't stop stuffing kiwi tarts in her face!' We just sat there, silent."

If you think that was awkward, you should've heard what was happening at the nine-story Palm Beach County jail that overlooks the third hole. "It hangs over that green," Pepper recalls. "Their rec area was on one of the upper floors. There was this one inmate who would climb up on the netting above. This guy was like Spiderman, just hanging way up on it. And he'd taunt the players the whole time, cat calls and all the usual gross stuff. I think they finally changed their P.T. time." Trump says this absolutely never happened, and then put up some very expensive tall trees to block the prison views.

No current or former LPGA commissioner would talk about Trump for this chapter, but when Trump was tweeting angrily on the day of Senator John McCain's dramatic Washington, D.C. funeral, former LPGA commissioner Carolyn Bivens (2005–2009) tweeted:

The depths of depravity know no bounds with Trump. Clueless and classless

Eventually, all good things must come to an end. After five years, the ADT tournament announced they'd be switching venues. Naturally, Trump sent them off with all best wishes.

"Just think," he said to a group of them that year, "next year at this time you'll be in a freaking Holiday Inn outside Houston."

When 33-time Tour winner Amy Alcott met Trump the first time, she was in the hotel elevator at the now-defunct Trump

Marina casino in New Jersey. She'd made an ace that day at an LPGA event and was beaming. Trump got in the elevator and recognized her.

"Are you a golfer?" he asked.

"Yeah, I'm Amy Alcott."

"Of course you are! I'm a big fan."

"Thanks! I actually had a hole in one today."

"Wow. That's fantastic. I'm going to have some champagne sent up."

"Wow. Thank you!"'

"Are you paying for your room?"

"Well, yes, of course."

"Well, you shouldn't be. We'll take care of it."

Alcott was flattered and thankful. Except no champagne ever arrived. And nobody ever took care of the room but her. "But I did see him leave in his helicopter," Alcott says.

They'd meet again when the LPGA held an event at his one-and-done Trump Los Angeles in Rancho Palos Verdes, California. "He'd put me in his cart," says Alcott. "And since it's Donald's cart, it goes twice as fast as any cart. We're driving down the middle of the freaking fairway DURING the tournament. One time, he goes, 'Oh, there goes Lorena Ochoa!' and he drove right down the middle of the fairway and up to the green. There was Ochoa trying to line up a birdie putt and he's waving and going, 'Hi Lorena! How you playing?'"

Longtime LPGA touring pro Kris Tschetter was even less impressed than Alcott. She and Trump played together in a

Wednesday Pro-Am once at the ShopRite Classic in New Jersey. "In my 25 years being a Tour pro," Tschetter says, "that was the worst experience I ever had playing golf."

Trump leered at her, spoke suggestively, and was "gross," Tschetter says. "He was just a pig. He hit on me, but in a kind of creepy way. I was SO not interested. I guess the fact I was married didn't matter to him. I was just like, 'Ewwwww' the rest of the round."

One of the other players in the group that day, a sales executive named Rob (he prefers not to give his last name), says it was worse than that. "Not only was he hitting on Kris, but Kris's husband was caddying! Trump would take me aside and go, 'What do you know about Kris and her husband?' I'm like, 'How should I know? He's right over there.'"

Since it was a tournament, he played by the rules, right?

"No, he kept taking all these extra shots," Tschetter says. "You can't do that in a Pro-Am. At one point, we made a 5 (as a team) and he said to write down a 4 because 'everybody cheats in Pro-Ams.' I mean, he couldn't be stopped. There was no way to say 'no' to him."

Rob: "I kept saying to him, 'Why are you cheating? To win an umbrella?' I wouldn't do it, so he took over the scorecard."

But here's the amazing thing about that day. After all the boorishness, Trump sent his helicopter to take them on a tour of New York, land on the roof of one of his buildings, wait while they ate dinner below, and bring them back to New Jersey, all on him. He wasn't even there.

It's not the money, it's the winning.

*   *   *

Just because the LPGA was done with him didn't mean Trump was done with the ladies. He lobbied for and got the 2017 U.S. Women's Open at Bedminster. The deal was signed long before he ran for president, and when he did, his first comment accused Mexico of sending us mostly rapists. Then came the *Access Hollywood* tape in which he boasts to Billy Bush about "grabbing women by the pussy." Then came the debate question from Fox's Megyn Kelly asking him why he has called women "slobs," "dogs," and "fat pigs."

LPGA and USGA officials stewed. How could they hold a women's Open hosted by a man whose idea of women came from *Porky's 6*? It was like riding a lion. They'd get eaten alive if they stayed on, but they'd get eaten alive if they didn't. They decided to just hold the tournament and hope for the best.

Immediately, women's groups started applying heat. A month before it was to start, a group called UltraViolet rented a plane and flew a banner over the *men's* U.S. Open that year that read: "USGA/LPGA: TAKE A MULLIGAN, DUMP TRUMP."

(*Aside to Greenpeace: Please call UltraViolet from now on for all golf-banner wording.*)

Women's pro golf was finally getting some press, just all the wrong kind. Media rooms at normally ignored LPGA events were filling up with reporters, all wanting to ask the players, "How do you feel about playing the Open at Donald Trump's golf course?"

American Brittany Lincicome shrugged and said, "Hopefully maybe he doesn't show up."

It'd be a great slogan, wouldn't it?

The 2017 U.S. Women's Open: Hopefully, Trump won't show up.

But he did show up. He drove past hundreds of protesters outside the gate and became the first U.S. president to ever attend a U.S. Women's Open. He sat in a corporate tent on the 18th green behind bulletproof glass and waved a lot. The Open was won by South Korean Park Sung-hyun, as if anybody remembers in the midst of the Trump Tornado.

When it was over, he tweeted:

Thank you to all of the supporters, who far out-numbered the protesters, yesterday at the Women's U.S. Open. Very cool!

One last note: Through the first 22 months of his presidency, there wasn't a single documented round when he'd played golf with a woman.

14

WHO'S YOUR CADDIES?

If a caddy can help you, you don't know how to play golf.
—DAN JENKINS

THE MOST LOYAL EMPLOYEE Donald J. Trump has doesn't work in the White House or on his campaign or on his legal team. The most faithful man in the president's life is his caddy at Trump Washington, a 60-something ex-Marine named A.J.

A.J. (he'd prefer we not use his last name) is so loyal that if you criticize Trump, he'll fight you—and has. One day, when the 2017 Senior PGA Championship was being held at Trump Washington, he overhead one of the Tour pro's caddies—Brian "Sully" Sullivan—dissing Trump.

"He was running his mouth, sir," says A.J., who calls everybody "sir" or "ma'am." "Yellin' about Mr. Trump. He was sayin' to somebody, 'Don't tell me how I have to feel about him! I hate that motherfucker!'"

A.J. says he came up on Sully from behind and put him in a full military choke hold, yelling, "Now, you listen to me, fucker! You're not gonna come to Mr. Trump's course and eat Mr. Trump's food and then use the word 'hate' about my president. I won't have it, you got me?"

That's not quite the way the story is told by Sullivan, who caddies for Senior Tour player Joe Durant, but his memory is a little fuzzy. "It's possible I was hungover," Sullivan recalls. "I don't like D.C. anyway and I sure as hell didn't want to be on a Trump course. Some guys started talking about Trump. I mentioned that I can't stand the son of a bitch. I said he was the biggest jerk in the world. A.J. got all worked up and said, 'That man pays my rent. He puts food on my table!' I said if he has to take money from that horse's ass, then he ought to find a different loop. He kind of just grumbled off. Of course, as luck would have it, he and I got paired for the first two days. We buried the hatchet."

Tensions were high because, for seniors, it was a big tournament and Trump's name was attached to it. There were protesters by the entrance every day that week, and A.J. always made sure to drive his car right by them. "There'd be a bunch a women out front with all their stupid signs, sir. So I go real slow by 'em, see, hit the window button—*zzzzzzttt*—toss 'em the bird and I yell, 'Fuck you!' They'd start yelling at me and I'm like—*zzzztttt*—right back up. And I laughed, sir."

A.J. sticks with Trump no matter how much it costs him. "I used to caddy for a lot of the ladies here, sir," he says. "But once Mr. Trump won the election, that all ended. Now I hardly do it at all, sir. I guess they don't like him. I'm the president's caddy and they're not gonna ask for me, sir. So that's it."

One time, after a bad drive, Trump slammed his driver back in his bag, as guys will do, and wasn't really watching what he was doing, and the driver ricocheted back and hit Trump in the head. "A.J.?" Trump asked, pissed. "Did you just hit me in the head with my own driver?"

"Sir, Mr. Trump, why would I do that?" A.J. said. "You're my president!"

There are more than a few members at Trump Washington who'd love to hit Trump in the head. A valet told me, "We had a bunch of them quit when he won." Most of the anti-Trump crowd stayed, but they resist in their own small ways. Every time one member sees A.J., he says, "Is this the day, A.J.? Is this the day?"

"Is this the day for what, sir?"

"Is this the day you take him out for me?"

"This one time, we're playing through, sir, like we do and, you know, usually the Secret Service has the people standing on the side in plenty of time for us. But this one guy, sir, young guy by the name of Jonathan Wallace, he was taking his sweet time getting out of the way. He was just moseying along, sir, doing it on purpose. Then he gives it one of these (A.J. flips the bird), right to Mr. Trump. Sir, that really made me mad. Mr. Trump just asked me who it was. I told him. He said, 'Let's go say hello.' Not me, sir. I went the other way. But Mr. Trump went over there and talked to him. Right away, this Wallace guy caved, sir. He caved." (I couldn't get Jonathan Wallace to call me back to hear his side of it.)

None of this used to be A.J.'s life. His Trump days used to be filled with pro athletes or businessmen. Now it's Congressmen and Fox hosts. Among his favorite these days is South Carolina senator Lindsey Graham, a Republican. "I love hearing that accent of his, sir. Mr. Trump plays pretty good with him. One time, he taught Mr. Trump a game called 'Hogan.' A Hogan is when you hit the fairway and the green and then two-putt. You do that, you get one Hogan point. So we played it, and, bam, Mr. Trump gets a Hogan on the first hole. And he just keeps going. Mr. Trump got 11 Hogans, sir! Shot 73 that day, I kid you not, sir. He made about four 15- to 20-foot putts on the back and shot 73. Coulda been even lower."

A one-over par 73 on a "wet and windy day" as Graham described it, for a 72-year-old overweight man? That's freaking unbelievable. How unbelievable? Well, at that same Senior PGA Championship, at the same course, from the same blue tees, Tom Watson never shot better than 74. Tom Kite put up a 75 and an 80. Corey Pavin had an 82. Between them, those three men have won nine majors.

When asked by a reporter how many gimmes there were in that 73, Graham allowed that they didn't really putt out that often and that "the president is better at receiving than giving." So, in other words, that 73 had more sugar in it than a family pack of Butterfingers. Now why would Graham resort to telling the truth about Trump's scorekeeping skills? Perhaps because of the vitriol Trump tweeted about him during the 2016 campaign, calling him "nasty" and "so easy to beat" and a man with "no honor."

Now, though, Graham is No. 1 on Trump's golf speed dial.

Graham remembers legendary Republican Senator John McCain asking him why he kept playing golf with someone like Trump. "I told him, 'I hope you understand....The best place to talk to him is in his world.'"

A.J. had Trump and Tennessee Republican senator Bob Corker in his world one day—along with no less than QB Peyton Manning—but it didn't seem to grease any wheels for his boss in Congress. Not long afterward, Corker said Trump needed "adult daycare."

A.J. has no time for another Republican senator, Kentucky's Rand Paul, whom he calls "a real chooch."

A chooch?

"Yeah, I don't know how to translate it, sir. A chooch. He treated me like a peon. Never even tried to fix a ballmark. Treated me like dirt, sir. He's a rich guy who thinks he's above everybody. A real chooch, sir." (Paul didn't return calls.)

Paul didn't sound like he had that much fun playing with Trump and A.J., either. When asked who won the golf match, Paul said, "The President never loses, didn't you know?"

Actually, yes, that's been mentioned.

In my 18 holes with A.J., he didn't say a single negative thing about Trump. He didn't even say a neutral thing about Trump. To hear A.J. tell it, Trump has Einstein's brain, Lincoln's wit, and Nightingale's heart. A.J. is smart that way. A loyal caddy can go a long, long way with Donald Trump.

Take Dan Scavino.

Scavino was a 16-year-old summer caddy when he got Trump's bag one day in 1990 at Briar Hall Golf and Country Club (NY), which was to become Trump Westchester. "I'll never forget the day his limo first pulled up," Scavino told *Westchester Magazine*. "I was star-struck. I remember his first gratuity. It was two bills—two hundred-dollar bills. I said, 'I am never spending this money.' I still have both bills."

The two hit it off. Trump told him, "You're gonna work for me one day." Scavino graduated from State University of New York (Plattsburgh) in 1998 and went to work for Coca-Cola, but Trump brought him back soon enough to be the assistant general manager at Westchester. Then Scavino became executive vice president. When Trump decided to run for president, Scavino asked if he could be part of it. Trump made him social media director of the campaign.

A billionaire and a caddy is a friendship that could only be made in golf, where kings take orders from cobblers and lifetime allegiances are sealed over 6 irons. It was the perfect match. Scavino is Trump's Mini Me. They both speak fluent golf. They both love stirring up liberals. They are both often very short on details and understanding, but long on Atomic Pile Driver slams and face-first personal takedowns. "They share thumbs," former campaign advisor Barry Bennett says. "They complete each other's tweets." Neither is well read nor a particularly good speller. Doesn't matter. As a two-man Twitter team, they shout from the rooftops anyway. They find a phrase—"fake news" or "enemy of the people" or "Crooked Hillary"—and repeat it so many times, people start to accept it.

With Scavino running Trump's feed, Trump's tweets became

even more bombastic, ultra-opinionated, and, often, a par 5 over the line. Former White House communications czar Hope Hicks called Scavino "the conductor of the Trump Train." One day, the train jumped the tracks. Trump tweeted out an image of Hillary Clinton, with a Star of David, against a background of money and the line "Most corrupt candidate ever!" It was a Scavino special, cobbled together with cut-and-paste images from the Internet and no thought of maybe asking somebody, "Hey, is this too much?"

Within seconds, Trump was blasted as antisemitic. Scavino had to issue a statement taking responsibility. He tweeted:

> **The social media graphic used this weekend was not created by the campaign. It was lifted from an Anti-Hillary Twitter user. The sheriff's badge, which is available under Microsoft shapes, fit the theme of corrupt Hillary and that is why I selected it.**

Except it wasn't a sheriff's badge, it was a Jewish star. (It was probably a mistake on Scavino's part, since his wife is Jewish.) The more Scavino pumped up Trump's tweets, the more it sounded like the Twitter feed of somebody else—Scavino's. For instance, on March 2, 2016, Scavino tweeted on his own account:

> **@MittRomney, You will not stop the #TrumpTrain You look like a complete LOSER. Very DESPERATE attempt. #Fail**

Hmmm. That's got a certain ring to it. Another time, just days before the election, Scavino tweeted:

NBC news is #FakeNews and more dishonest than even CNN. They are a disgrace to good reporting. No wonder their news ratings are way down!

A minute later, the same message, word for word, was posted on Trump's account as his original tweet. Scavino hastily deleted his, but in a world of screenshots, it was too late.

Robert Draper, of the *New York Times Magazine*, conducted an exhaustive study of Trump's tweets and estimated that Scavino was "responsible for—at least as a 'co-conspirator' "—about half of Trump's 37,000 tweets. The late-night and early-morning tweets seem to be 100% Trump, but the daytime stuff has the patina of Scavino. Whichever it is, neither of them particularly knows what they're doing. Scavino violated the Hatch Act by tweeting support for a candidate. Scavino also got Trump dragged to Federal District Court by blocking some followers, which, it turns out, is unconstitutional for an American president.

Still, he's put Trump's Twitter rants on a kind of steroid regimen. Fox News host Megyn Kelly accused Scavino of rabble-rousing against her: "The vast majority of Donald Trump supporters are not at all this way," Kelly told an audience in Washington. "It's that far corner of the Internet that really enjoys nastiness and threats and unfortunately there is a man who works for Donald Trump whose job it is to stir these people up and that man needs to stop doing that. His name is Dan Scavino."

But just think of it: Trump's Twitter feed is the most powerful pulpit on the globe, and a caddy has his hands on it, daily. It's full-throated Trumpness, even Trumpier than Trump, sent without censure or concern and teeming with what Bush 41 called Trump's "casual cruelty." It's a flamethrower that sometimes winds up setting the Oval Office curtains on fire. During his 2012 campaign, Mitt Romney had 22 people approve each tweet before it went out. During the day, Trump has two—himself and his caddy. At night, just one. That's not going to change. CNN asked Scavino, who is now the White House Director of Communications, if there was anything Trump could do or say that would make him leave Trump's side. He answered with an unequivocal "no."

Scavino refused my requests to interview him, but we know he's a Catholic who once kissed the pope's ring. He was about 40 when Trump was elected. Scavino's wife, Jennifer, became sick with Lyme disease, and the couple says they spent so much money trying to get her well, they went bankrupt in 2015. Some people say this is why they got divorced after 18 years. "Dan was a great husband, though," says Ian Gillule, who worked with him at Westchester. "He's very gregarious, a big personality, a people pleaser, and very political." Also, apparently, not a guy who will ask his billionaire boss for a loan.

In a way, A.J. and Scavino are the same guy. A.J. is Trump's outdoor caddy and Scavino his indoor one. They're both mostly unknown, yet they know all the secrets. They both do the same job: They give their man the right club to take shots with. These two work for a human flamethrower and yet somehow haven't been torched. Cabinet members, attorneys general, chiefs of staff come and go like the Wendy's drive-thru and yet they stay employed. What's their secret? It might be the Caddy Code: Show Up, Keep Up, Shut Up. It only takes one bad read or one bad club to get fired as a caddy, but A.J. has been Trump's loop for years now. Scavino has survived Trump's well-oiled guillotine and remains one of the few staffers who's lasted since the beginning. A president who trusts nobody trusts Scavino. "The president has zero concern that Dan has any interest in anything but serving him," the *New York Times* quoted a top administrator as saying. When you're the only other person who has the president's Twitter password, you're trusted.

All of which proves one thing. Jeff Sessions should've learned to caddy.

15

LITTLE BALL, BIG BALL

I'm not a schmuck. Even if the world goes to hell
in a handbasket, I won't lose a penny.
—Donald J. Trump

ONE DAY I WAS playing with my friend Lenny "Two Down" O'Connor. He kept hitting his irons "fat"—hitting the ground before he hit the ball. A good iron shot is just the opposite—the club traps the ball against the earth and sends it soaring.

"Two, you idiot!" he yelled at himself. "Little ball first, THEN big ball!"

That's been part of the problem with Donald Trump as president. In his brain, the big ball keeps getting in the way of the little ball and vice versa.

So many of the problems, controversies, and conflicts Trump has gotten into as president started with golf. Conversely, his golf has twisted how he makes decisions about this great, big, troubled blue ball he's supposed to be running.

Take, for instance, Puerto Rico.

Why did Trump seem to turn his back on our own people during the devastating 2017 hurricane that would leave almost 3,000 dead and the island without water and power for eight months?

Why? Golf might be why.

It started in 2008, when the Trump Organization agreed to operate a course called Coco Beach Golf & Country Club, about 30 minutes from San Juan. It was in trouble and needed a big name to get it some publicity. So, for a fat fee and part of the deal, Trump agreed to operate the course and let them call it Trump International Golf Club Puerto Rico. In his pitch to get the deal, Trump guaranteed the course would start turning a profit. Bigly. Puerto Ricans were thrilled.

But Trump only sunk it deeper. Before Trump, the course was losing about $5.4 million a year. With Trump—$6.3 million. Some of that was the $600,000 Trump took out for his fee over those years. Within three years, the Coco Beach company defaulted on $26 million in government bonds and had to get $33 million more in government financing, which they also couldn't repay. Trump finally declared bankruptcy on his end of the project in 2015, and the Coco group went belly up, too, leaving the Puerto Ricans with a $33 million hole.

Fast forward two years to the worst hurricane to hit Puerto Rico in 85 years. It was a catastrophe. Yet, as American citizens were dying for water, medicine, and power in Puerto Rico, their president seemed to not give a damn. He made jokes. "See, there's this big thing called the Atlantic Ocean," he said. He mused about how to pronounce the name "Puerto Rico." Then he decided they only had themselves to blame. He tweeted:

> **Texas & Florida are doing great but Puerto Rico, which was already suffering from broken infrastructure & massive debt, is in deep trouble.**

That was too much for Lainie Green, a Puerto Rican marketing executive who threw an epic tweetstorm back at him:

> **Massive debt you and your sons helped when you bankrupted your golf course & never paid back the $33 mil bond you left Puerto Ricans with.**

> **You remember because you filed for the bankruptcy a month after you started running for president in 2015.**

> **So how much are you going to give back of that $600,000 paycheck you got for sticking Puerto Rico with a $33 million debt?**

"He came down here and was so obnoxious," says Green. "He said, 'We're gonna pour $600 million into the course.' That was bullsh*t. They didn't put any of their own money into it. He and his sons were here for seven years and every year they lost more and more money. The [Coco] owners went to the [Puerto Rican] tourism bureau and asked for a $33 million bond. The government said no....But Trump's sons kept saying, 'No, Donald Trump will be here all the time! He knows what he's doing! Trust us!' So they loaned the money. By 2015, they had to declare bankruptcy and the Trumps left us holding the bag."

When Trump visited the devastated island in late September, he seemed cavalier about it all, almost flip, visiting only the mostly untouched ritzy part of the island, where he shot rolls of paper towels like 3-pointers at a room full of dismayed Puerto Ricans and then left.

"That was disgusting," Green remembers. (She was crying by now as she spoke.) "These are human beings. American citizens! The people he's responsible for! He had absolutely no empathy for our people. There's something psychotic and wrong about that. He had every opportunity to say, 'Hey, I love Puerto Rico. I don't want to fail them.' Instead he took swipes at my people and threw paper towels to his f*cking rich friends. I'd love to see Trump Tower without power for eight hours, much less eight months."

If she could get face-to-face with Trump, what would she say?

"I'd say, 'Would you ever leave your grandkids alone in the dark with no power, no water, and nothing to help them? Because that's what you did to these people.'...He let them die."

Take, for instance, immigration.

When Trump first tried banning U.S. travel to people from seven different Muslim countries—Iran, Iraq, Libya, Somalia,

Sudan, Syria, and Yemen—some Americans wondered, "Why those seven? Why not the UAE or Saudi Arabia? After all, the UAE helped fund the Taliban and may have been a backer of 9/11. Saudi Arabia has been the breeding ground for hundreds of terrorists, not to mention Osama Bin Laden."

Why? Golf might be why.

Even now, Trump is up to his clavicles in golf deals with the UAE, specifically controversial UAE tycoon Hussain Sajwani, sometimes called "The Donald of Dubai." Sajwani, a devout Muslim, even came to Trump's post-election party at Mar-a-Lago, earning a shout out from the man of the hour. "Hussain and the whole family, the most beautiful people, are here from Dubai tonight!" Sajwani owns two courses with Trump's name— Trump International Golf Club Dubai and Trump World Golf Club Dubai. The latter was designed by no less than Tiger Woods. Trump wasn't going to screw that up with a travel ban. What if Tiger needs to meet with his concrete guy?

Then there's China. Trump's relationship with China is fickle, but in June of 2018, Trump threw a lifeline to shady Chinese telecom giant ZTE. It got both aisles of Congress leaping out of their chairs in protest. "China…uses these telecom companies to spy & steal from us," Republican senator Marco Rubio pointed out. So why did Trump grease the skids for a company that America wants to see burn?

Why? Golf might be why.

At Trump Dubai, Sajwani awarded a $32 million infrastructure construction contract to the mostly state-owned China State Construction Engineering Corporation to build a road that would lead to the golf course. In other words, Trump was

suddenly in bed with China. So when China's Xi Jinping personally asked Trump for help with ZTE, Trump might've thought,
"Would helping ZTE make working with Xi really easy? Yes. Yes,
it would." So he did it, against the advice of nearly everybody.

And why, you ask, wasn't Indonesia on the travel-ban list, since
there are more Muslims in Indonesia than any country in the
world (227 million) and, in just the first three weeks of May 2018,
49 people died in multiple ISIS attacks there committed by Indone-
sian Muslims?

Why? Golf might be why.

Trump has two courses about to open in Indonesia, one in
Bali, to be redesigned by Phil Mickelson, and the other in Jakarta,
by four-time major winner Ernie Els. Remember when Trump's
lawyers announced they'd be suspending all unfinished projects
now that he was president? Not so much. He's moved forward in
Indonesia. Should an American president be in business at all in
a country like Indonesia, whose citizens committed almost twice
as many terrorist acts as Iran in 2016? Depends. Will this country put up a golf course with his name on it?

When Trump made "Buy American, Hire American" one of
his campaign slogans, he was at the same time issuing an executive order that greatly increased the amount of foreign H-2B temporary visa workers coming to this country. But why would he
do that when an H-2B could come here and join a terrorist cell as
easily as somebody who hopped a fence or faked a passport?

Why? Golf might be why.

Trump needs H-2B visa workers to make his golf courses
and hotels work. He knows this country doesn't have an

unemployment problem. It has an employment problem. It can't find enough people to do jobs most Americans won't do—mowing fairways, cleaning hotel rooms, washing gold-rimmed soup bowls. So nobody in golf was surprised that three days after the Trump administration raised the H-2B visa cap from 66,000 per year to 81,000, the Trump Organization applied for and got an additional 76 of them to use at its properties.

You ask, "Does Trump employ illegal immigrants at his golf courses?"

I answer, "Did Liz Taylor own a wedding dress?"

In December of 2018, Trump Bedminster got caught employing an illegal maid, to almost nobody's surprise. "They had all kinds of illegal immigrants working at Doral," says Joe Santilli, a former member there. "I know because I'd talk to them. I speak Spanish. They would be hired through a contractor so Trump wasn't on the line if they got caught. But they had tons of illegals working on crews there."

There's almost no conceivable way not to. I don't know many golf clubs that don't use them. The day I played with Trump at Westchester, he stopped three laborers who were finishing up a cart path and gave them each $100 bills for their good work. Then he got back in the cart and said, "Now they're the Donald Trumps of Chile!"

Take, for instance, Cuba.

When Trump got into office, he immediately started reversing Obama orders that would finally allow Americans to travel to Cuba, calling it a "bad deal" for Americans. In one iteration of the travel ban, Cuba was even named to his hit list. Some Americans thought, "Why? Why come down against Cuba now after all the progress the two countries have made?"

Why? Golf might be why.

In 1998, according to *Newsweek*, Trump secretly looked into building a hotel and golf course in Cuba. He paid an American consulting firm called Seven Arrows Investment to travel to Cuba to explore his options there, in direct violation of the embargo on Americans doing business in Cuba. Seven Arrows charged Trump $68,000 for the trip but, to disguise its illegality, made it look like a charity trip.

It went deeper. According to *Bloomberg*, more than a few Trump Organization people went down to Cuba to explore golf course and hotel possibilities more recently, too. When *Bloomberg* found out, it asked Eric Trump about it. He emailed back: "While we are not sure whether Cuba represents an opportunity for us, it is important for us to understand the dynamics of the markets that our competitors are exploring."

Wait, is that a denial?

There's paperwork for all this—lying to the IRS, repeatedly violating the embargo—but the statute of limitations has passed, so why let a bunch of snoopy American reporters in there to dig up new stuff? Trump may have thought, "Let's just keep everybody out of Cuba altogether."

Take, for instance, the wall.

Not *that* wall—the wall he wants to build in Ireland to keep the Atlantic Ocean off his Irish golf course, Doonbeg.

"The sea water is clearly rising," Trump's attorneys argued in a planning application in Doonbeg, a little burg on the southwest coast of Ireland. "Mr. Trump's property stands to be forever damaged without the wall." It said it right there in the application. The Trump Organization was asking for permission to build a giant wall because the effects of "climate change" were wrecking Trump's course.

Imagine that. Trump, who has said climate change is "a hoax," "fictional," and "a canard," was asking for the right to protect himself against rising sea water. The man who pulled the U.S. out of the Paris Agreement on climate change believes climate change is damaging his property.

"In our view, it could reasonably be expected that the rate of sea level rise might become twice of that presently occurring," the application said. Trump actually wanted two "flood defense walls," as his lawyers called them. Combined, they'd run about 3,000 feet along the coast, protecting three golf holes.

The Council gave permission. Irish environmentalists flipped out. They agreed the sea was rising, but said a wall could open a Pandora's box of ecological problems. For one thing, it would push all the water onto nearby farms, ruining their crops. The beach and dunes could be destroyed. Surfer groups opposed it. As of the start of 2019, the application was still under appeal.

A bit of advice to the world's leaders: If you want to get in good with Trump, take golf lessons.

Japan's prime minister Shinzō Abe gets golf. He gave Trump

a $3,755 gold-plated driver. They play together often. Chinese president Xi Jinping, though, hates golf. He's shut down 111 golf courses in China already and forbids any of the 88 million members of his Communist Party to play it. He thinks golf is a waste of water and land. Whatever good Trump did for their relationship with ZTE, Xi's disgust for golf hurts it. Would Trump start a trade war with China out of the blue, just to get even?

If you run a country but don't play golf, you're pretty much dead to Trump. German chancellor Angela Merkel always seems to be on the outside, her nose pressed to the grill room window, looking in at Trump and the day's foursome. One German official publicly suggested she should learn to play golf.

Playing golf hasn't hurt members of Trump's golf clubs any. Trump has put at least five of his members into senior roles in his administration, including Newt Gingrich's wife, Callista, America's new ambassador to the Vatican, and Adolfo Marzol—member at Trump Washington—who is now the senior adviser at the Department of Housing and Urban Development.

Andrew Giuliani, son of Trump's lawyer Rudy Giuliani, was named in March to a White House post as public liaison assistant. He's a scratch golfer and member at Trump Westchester. Robin Bernstein might seem an odd choice to be the ambassador to the Dominican Republic, seeing as she only speaks "basic Spanish," until you realize she was a campaign donor, sells insurance to Trump, and is a founding member at Mar-a-Lago. Whenever she's in the D.R., she can check in on Trump's proposed golf courses as Cap Cana, another unfinished project he was supposedly going to suspend and didn't.

Doesn't every president appoint their friends to sweet jobs? Yes, but unlike any president before him, Trump never divested his businesses before becoming president. Every single decision he makes as POTUS can affect his own wallet. When you can get up to $350,000 from people for joining your club, it helps to make membership attractive.

Hey, how would you like to be ambassador to Sweden? Just sign here!

The lines get blurred. In 2018, Trump visited the factory of avid golfer Robert Mehmel, a man who sells millions of dollars' worth of radars and electronics to the U.S. military and who also happens to be a member of Trump's Bedminster golf club.

CSPAN captured Kevin Burke, a lobbyist for airports, mentioning to Trump at a White House meeting, "I'm a member of your club, by the way."

"Very good, very good," Trump replied.

The word is out. If you're a lobbyist, a special-interest dealer, a foreign intermediary who needs Trump's ear, pony up the initiation fee and join one of his clubs. The access is fantastic. Can't afford that? Have a wedding there. As advertised for a time on a Trump Bedminster brochure, if you hold your wedding there, Trump might even show up, say hello, and pose for pictures, at no additional charge. ("We ask you and your guests to be respectful of his time & privacy," the brochure asked.) Lots of people have posted videos of him doing exactly that. On July 2, 2018, Trump surprised a wedding, posed for pictures, and even kissed the bride. Then he walked off to applause and a cry of "We love you!"

Somewhere, a tiny tear trickled down Angela Merkel's cheek.

*   *   *

For most people, it's the goats.

When I try to explain how Trump constantly hot-foots his golf cart down the line between illegal and immoral, I always bring up the goats.

"Did you know," I say, "that on Trump's Bedminster course there's a small herd of eight goats?"

Goats?

"Goats," I say. "He keeps eight goats on his golf course in order to get a farmland tax break, saving him about $80,000 in taxes per year. He also has a tiny hay-making enterprise at Trump Colts Neck in New York, just enough to get another farmland write-off."

Wait. Our current president keeps goats on a golf course as a tax dodge?

"Yes. Goats. To get an $80,000 tax dodge. A man who costs Americans nearly $4 million every time he goes to visit his golf course in Florida has found a way to save $80,000 in taxes."

That is so…genius!

They don't know the half of it. Even as president, Trump and his family have mixed shrewdness and self-dealing, politics and golf into a kind of not-quite-illegal but odorous machine that lets them get what they want.

Take the helicopter pad Trump uses at Mar-a-Lago, his winter refuge. Trump pestered and yelled and bullied the powers that be in West Palm Beach to let him land his helicopter on his property, but he was always denied. Hell, in West Palm Beach, the waiters have helicopters. But when Trump became president, he insisted he needed the pad to land Marine One. National security. The town said okay, but only for as long as he was president and only for Marine One. Great. Trump built the chopper pad. One week later, Trump's personal chopper, with a giant TRUMP painted on the side of it, was parked on the pad.

Before he entered office, LBJ put his radio and TV stations into a blind trust. Jimmy Carter sold his peanut farm. Both Clinton and Bush 43 put their businesses in blind trusts. Obama took his entire stock portfolio and put it in Treasury bonds. Not Trump. He didn't change a thing except to say that "Don and Eric and Ivanka will be running things." As a result, every time Trump plays golf at his courses in West Palm, Bedminster, or Washington, he's putting money in his own pocket with free advertising, not to mention the cost of housing and feeding all that staff. (Staff even gets a discount in his pro shops.)

If you thought Trump wouldn't dare use the Office of the President to try to get what he wants for his golf courses, you don't know Trump. It took only a few days after the election to prove it. That's when he took a congratulatory meeting in Trump Tower with four Brits—two money guys who'd backed Brexit, a journalist from the right-wing journalist site Breitbart UK, and the very vocal pro-Brexit activist Nigel Farage. One of the Brits, Andy Wigmore, returned to London and told the BBC that Trump kept complaining about the windmills Scotland was putting up in the sea next to his Aberdeen course. (Maybe you heard: Trump really hates those windmills.)

Wigmore quoted Trump as saying, over and over again, "They offend me." He said Trump begged them all to go back to the UK and try to do something "about getting rid of the wind farms."

It got worse. When the BBC interview aired, the journalist from Breitbart, Raheem Kassam, immediately emailed Wigmore, according to CNN, and flipped out:

WHY DID YOU GIVE THOSE QUOTES. This was a PRIVATE MEETING AND YOU HAVE F*** ALL OF US NOW.**

Kassam insisted Wigmore say the conversation "never happened," an odd demand coming from a journalist. White House Spokeswoman Hope Hicks said Trump never brought up wind farms at all. Then CNN showed her the emails. Ooops.

Try as they have, nobody has been able to get Trump to divorce his golf businesses interests from the country's interests. In fact, Trump mixes them all the time. Since he has stayed at one of his properties roughly one-third of his days as president, American taxpayer dollars stuff his pockets, unchecked. In pursuit of them, he has no problem doling out free advertising for his golf properties. In an address to the South Korean National Assembly, Trump managed to get in a plug for how great his Bedminster course was. In an address of the U.S. Coast Guard, he made sure to mention that his Trump International is "one of the great courses of the world." On his 55-million-follower Twitter feed, he's raved about how "amazing" this course is or "magical" that one is or "spectacular" a third one is. A woman named

Dani Bostick, a schoolteacher and Army wife from Winchester, Virginia, noticed it, too. On July 15, 2017, she called him out on it via Twitter:

Nice job sneaking Bedminster into the caption of the picture. Nothing like free advertising on your huge social media account.

Apparently, Trump didn't appreciate that. She got blocked.

Trump has found a way to cash in on the presidency like nobody who came before him. For instance, just in golf:

- Did it seem unusual to you that a few weeks after Trump was inaugurated, he doubled the initiation fee at Mar-a-Lago from $100,000 to $200,000? Then again, why wouldn't he? Suddenly, hanging around places like Mar-a-Lago, Bedminster, and Trump Washington gives an ambitious CEO or lobbyist fabulous access to the most powerful man in the world. Using the GHIN handicap system and membership rolls, *USA Today* found that at least 50 executives of companies that have federal contracts, plus 21 lobbyists and trade-group officials, are members at the clubs Trump visits the most often in Florida, Virginia, and New Jersey. Two-thirds of them played on one of the 58 days the president was there, *USA Today* reported.
- Does it seem odd that a guy who promised to have "absolutely no conflict of interest with his businesses" continues to lord over those businesses? Former hockey star Mike Eruzione belongs to Trump Jupiter and sees it. "I talk to our pro [David

Trout] a lot," Eruzione says. "He [Trump] is very hands on. He calls and checks on how it's doing, asks about certain greens, how the fairways are, where to move this or that, even though he's the president. He's a very hands-on guy."

Oops. Five minutes for blabbing.

- Did it seem funny that the very day he met with the Queen of England at Windsor Castle, he flew directly to his Trump Turnberry golf course in Scotland, plugging it shamelessly on Twitter? "This place is incredible!" he wrote. He only had two days to prepare for his historic meeting with Russian president Vladimir Putin in Helsinki. Why wouldn't he go there and start cramming? Maybe because Helsinki doesn't have a Trump golf course to market?

Trump gets a lot of deserved credit for what he did in the world of golf during The Great Recession of 2007. Then, golf was radioactive. People were leaving the game by the busload. A bank would rather help you buy a yacht than buy a golf course. But Trump went out and started buying golf courses with cash everywhere—five along the American east coast and three more in Scotland and Ireland. But where would a guy coming off four bankruptcies get that much cash to buy all those courses? And why was the self-proclaimed King of Debt paying cash?

Some thought it had to be the Russians. They might've gotten ten that idea from his son, Eric, who, in 2014, told golf writer James Dodson, "We don't rely on American banks. We have all the funding we need out of Russia.... We've got some guys that really, really love golf, and they're really invested in our programs. We just go there all the time."

Congress followed up on those comments but never came up with anything. Since Trump won't release his tax returns, it's nearly impossible to know. So whence then?

Allow me to take an educated guess.

When you join any private golf club owned by one person— like Trump's are—you must plunk down a fat initiation fee, which can run from $50,000 to $500,000. Trump Westchester gets $200,000. Trump Bedminster gets $350,000. You get your money back when you leave, as long as there's a new person in line willing to take your place and pay the going initiation fee. (Don't get ahead of me here.)

Let's say, just for the math, Trump Covfefe has 500 members, all of whom have put down $75,000 each. That's $37.5 million in cash sitting in the bank. Most course owners save that money in case there's a disaster at the course, i.e., moto-cross vandals hold an impromptu night-time event on your fairways or a massive flood hits that you're not covered for. But not Trump. He keeps those fat fees. When you look at the contracts that Trump has his members sign, you notice the fine print says, "Membership deposits and all other club revenues are the property of the owner of the club and may be used for any purpose, in its sole discretion."

It means Trump can legally take that $37.5 million of those Covfefe dues and do whatever he wants to with it. He can buy hair dye with it. He can corner the ketchup market. Or he can buy golf courses. Lots and lots of golf courses.

According to the *Washington Post*, Trump spent $400 million on golf courses, wineries, and hotels between 2006 and 2015, all in cash. "It's not unethical," says National Golf Course Owners Association CEO Jay Karen. "It's in the contract. But to me, it's a risk. If something happens and you need that money for the course, it's not there."

Sorry, folks. I know the Bolivian wombats ate the entire course, but all your money is in my fabulous course in Ireland. You should come see it!

Or let's say the bottom falls out of the economy and Trump wants to sell Trump Covfefe for $50 million, but he can't get anywhere near that. Let's say he can only get $5 million for it. The new owner buys the club AND the initiation fees, so they better be there.

Remember when he informed the Trump Jupiter members that their refundable deposits were suddenly nonrefundable? Is it possible he'd already used their deposits to buy another course and he didn't have it?

Could this little maneuver also be what Trump referred to throughout 2018 when he alleged that special counsel Robert Mueller was "horribly conflicted" in his investigation of Trump and Russia? Mueller, then the FBI director, quit Trump D.C. in 2011—two years after Trump bought it—with no hard feelings, Mueller's spokesman says. But the *Washington Post* reported Mueller quit the club and then "sent a letter requesting a dues refund in accordance with normal club practice and never heard back." Trump said this was "a huge conflict of interest" and meant the investigation was tainted. It wasn't much money. Most people paid about $40,000 to get in. "He probably didn't get his money back," says Trump D.C. member Ned Scherer, "but I don't know anybody that's gotten their money back since Trump bought it."

It's all legal, but it also means he's got a kind of golfing Ponzi scheme going: The money could be long spent, but it doesn't matter because Mr. X, who is leaving, gets his deposit back from Mr. Y, who is coming. Trump never has to reach into his pocket. It all works great—until something really bad happens, like an infestation of glowworms ruins all your greens and you didn't buy glowworm insurance.

Whenever I talk to people who belong to Trump courses but hate Trump, they always say the same thing: "I'm just here to play golf. It's got nothing to do with Trump. I'd never support him personally."

Memo to them: When you forked over your $200,000, it went right in his pocket.

Trump as president is baffling to the political world, but to we golfers, he speaks our language. Often, he speaks it at the excruciatingly wrong time, but he speaks it.

For instance, when 17 people were murdered at Stoneman Douglas High School in Florida, Trump wanted teachers to start packing guns in class. But not just any teachers. "I want highly trained people that have a natural talent...like hitting a golf ball...or putting....How come some people always make the 4-footer and some people, under pressure, can't even take their club back!"

STAFFER: Mr. President, there's been yet another mass murder in our schools!

TRUMP: Find me a good putter!

Of his dalliances with the Kremlin, Trump once said, "This
Russia stuff is nasty business. Much nastier than trying to make
a three-foot putt."

For the rest of the world, it's an ethical horror show, but for
his golf buddies, Trump as president is a hoot. A friend of mine
is tight with Trump. Has been forever. Talks to him once a week.
He wouldn't speak on the record, but he summed it up like this:
"Look, The Donald is The Donald. He's fun. He's nuts. He's full
of shit. He'll probably go down as the worst president of all time,
but he'll always be a friend of mine."

Trump's pal, architect Tom Fazio, says the world takes Trump
way too seriously. "I love that Donald will say anything. I mean,
anything! He just shoots from the hip and crazy stuff comes out.
He's always been like that. But the press thinks he's serious. He's
usually not serious."

But...but...but...we're talking about nukes, climate change,
refugees, guns, Russia, China, war, the future of the nation, and
the future of life on this big ball. Maybe it's time he got a little
serious?

Neither Trump nor anybody with the Trump Organization
would talk to me or take my questions for this book. But maybe
the whole problem with Trump's presidency is golf itself. Golf
is a solitary game. In golf, it's just you and that great big course

waiting with all its perils and traps. But to run the world, you need teammates. Trump hates teammates. That's one reason he loves golf so much. He's always in a cart by himself, 100 yards ahead of everybody else, just Him and his caddy, the better to kick and throw and foozle. But you can't kick and throw and foozle your way through a presidency. You can't cheat and fudge and fake running the world, for one good reason:

You don't own the course.

16

THE STAIN

Remember, Ricky, golf is a gentleman's sport.
—JACK REILLY

WHEN JAPAN SURRENDERED AT the end of World War II, my Army lieutenant dad was assigned to duty in Tokyo. He'd heard that Emperor Hirohito played golf. So he went to the Imperial Palace and knocked on the guard house door. When they asked what he wanted, he said, "Well, I wondered if the emperor might like to play golf with me this afternoon."

That's how it's always been in my family. Golf solves everything. Our very bones are made of balata. The whole family golfs—nieces, nephews, uncles, aunts, nearly every single one of us. I can remember, when I was six years old, my mom, dad, and brother being on the pages of the sports section because they all were playing in the same tournament. I have an aunt who still wins her flight and she's 91. We have a giant nine-hole family tournament every year—The Reilly Roundup—and everybody wears a yellow shirt, just like the one we buried my dad in.

So when a man like President Donald Trump pees all over the game I love, lies about it, cheats at it, and literally drives tire tracks all over it, it digs a divot in my soul and makes me want to march into the Oval Office, grab him by that long red tie, and yell, "Stop it!"

You can think Trump has made America great again. You can think Trump has made America hate again. But there's one thing I know: He's made golf terrible again.

We were just getting past the stereotype of golf being a game for fat, blowhard, rich white guys playing on fenced-off courses while people of color push lawnmowers behind them—and along comes Trump.

We were just getting people out of their stupid golf carts and back to walking, the way golf is best—when along comes Trump, a man who believes exercise only leads to death, who *never* walks when he plays, even in defiance of his walk-only rules at Turnberry and Aberdeen.

We were just getting millennials to think golf was cool again with stylish, athletic players like Tiger and Jordan Spieth and Lexi Thompson—when along comes Trump in his 1990 Dockers ready to bust at the seam playing overwatered, gold-doorknob golf courses with all his cronies, making golf about as cool as Depends and leaving a big orange stain on the game we may never get out.

Trump treats golf like it's some sort of reward for being rich. In fact, that's *exactly* what he thinks. "I'd like to see golf be an aspirational game," he has said more than once, "where you aspire to join a club someday, you want to play, you go out and become successful. That's the way I feel."

Enjoy bowling, poor people! Sucks to be you.

He said it to a *Golf Digest* reporter once, and the reporter was flabbergasted. He replied, "So you'd like [golf] to be an elitist activity?"

Trump: "It was always meant to be, and people get there through success."

No, that's *never* what it was meant to be. It was a game invented in Scotland by shepherds. In Scotland, it's still a game of the people. It's available and affordable to everybody from the blue bloods who live in the stately mansions to the rough hands who laid the bricks. At most golf clubs in Scotland, you finish your round, tip your caddy, then drink with him at the bar afterward. He's a member.

Golf in America isn't the least bit Trumpy, either. The average price of four hours of fresh-air fun in America is $35, according to the National Golf Foundation. It's too wonderful a game to confine to any one set of people. Ninety percent of golfers play primarily at public courses. Golf is for everybody of any age, race, or bank account. So what's wrong with that? Okay, they'll never have white Rolls-Royces or solid-gold telescopes, but why can't they have golf?

"Any golf, any place, any time is going to do a soul good," Ben Crenshaw once told me. "It's not just for the rich. Golf is for everybody. Golf makes a difference in people's lives. It doesn't matter who you are, young and old, rich or poor, it's a game that you can stay with the rest of your life. There aren't many games like that."

Golf should be aspirational? That's not what Arnold Palmer thought. The son of a club pro, Arnie brought golf to the plumbers and the typists.

Golf is a reward for making money? That's not what Tiger Woods thinks, either. The son of a Vietnam vet, the first black winner of the Masters, he's opened up the game to hundreds of millions of people.

Golf is a reward for success? That's not what The First Tee thinks. It gives low-income kids a chance to learn golf's gifts of skill, manners, and friendship, for free. Ask Tom Watson. You go to his house and his trophy cases are mostly empty. They're on loan to The First Tee.

If golf was only for country club kids, the world would've never known Sam Snead, Ben Hogan, Byron Nelson, Arnie, Seve Ballesteros, Tiger Woods, Michelle Wie, and 100 other great players.

But here's where Trump is killing my game: Only 8.5% of Americans play golf, which means 91.5% don't really know what it's about. They don't get the jubilation of watching a little ball that was just *sitting there* a few seconds ago rocket off against a bright blue sky to a target 300 yards away no wider than a broomstick. They don't get that 18 briskly walked holes carrying your bag is a joyous way to work out. They've never known the feeling of laughing with three friends all afternoon so hard that you just *gotta* go an emergency 9. How many of that 91.5% won't even try the game now because of Trump? How many more will listen to his blowhard golf bragging and hear about his shameless cheating and avoid golf like bed bugs?

Most people want to grow the game. Double Down wants to shrink it. "It shouldn't be a game for all strata of society," he once said. "It should be aspirational. By getting away from it, it actually hurt golf."

No, what's hurting golf is Trump.

You might be thinking, "What does golf have to do with being president? What does it matter that he cheats at it? What's it got to do with leading the country?"

Everything.

If you'll cheat to win at golf, is it that much further to cheat to win an election? To turn a Congressional vote? To stop an investigation?

If you'll lie about every aspect of the game, is it that much further to lie about your taxes, your relationship with Russians, your groping of women?

If you're adamant that that the poor don't deserve golf, is it that much further to think they don't deserve health care, clean air, safe schools?

I'm glad my dad didn't live to see a Commander in Cheat like Trump. It would've turned his stomach. Somebody who wins club championships from the next state is not a gentleman. Somebody who makes his caddies cheat for him to earn their tip is not a gentleman. Somebody who bullies and manipulates and yells that his courses are the best in the world when that world absolutely knows otherwise is not a gentleman.

I feel sorry for Donald Trump. I feel sorry for someone who has to juggle that many spinning lies, who has to fight that many endless feuds, who has to cheat and lie and insult so many good people just to stand on a rickety first-place podium that never stops needing rebuilding. How exhausting must that be?

The truth is, the person in golf Donald Trump cheats the most is himself. He's cheating himself of the joy, the endless challenge, golf brings. Every golfer who loves the game loves it for the battle it brings within himself—*Can I rise up to be as good as I want to be today?* In life, we're defined by the obstacles we overcome. That's the stuff we hang on our inner wall. But if you cheat to get around those obstacles, you never know the thrill of actually beating them.

It's like buying a trophy in a pawn shop. You can shine it up and show it off and pretend you won it, but when you get close to it, it only reflects the face of a loser.

Acknowledgments

I'm deeply grateful to Mauro DiPreta, who believed in this from the get-go and took it 93% of the way, through no fault of his own. *Non posso aspettare i tesori tu trovare prossimo, amico.*

Thanks, also, to my terrific researcher and tiny-shoulder-to-lean-on, Marianne (Moose) Moore, who was always there for me, no matter what giant cyclops she was having to slay at the same time. You are the strongest little person I've ever met.

A large debt of gratitude goes to some terrific friends and reporters in the golf-writing dodge, most especially John Huggan, Jeff Babineau, Michael Bamberger, Jaime Diaz, Alan Shipnuck, Stephanie Wei, Geoff Shackleford, Eamon Lynch, et al. If you'd ever stop working and come to the bar, I owe you each a cold beer.

Thanks to Gwenda Blair, Trump's biographer, who kept

taking my endless calls with kindness. If you were grinding your teeth, I never heard it.

Thanks very much to my fabulous pit-bull agent and life-long friend, Janet Pawson. (Good luck to us!) And thanks to the whole squadron of terrific and smart people who pushed this thing over the finish line: Sarah Falter, David Lamb (sorry about my damn laptop), Michael Barrs, and Odette Fleming.

Mostly, though, thanks and all my love to TLC, The Lovely Cynthia, who put up with a book that consumed me like a raging wildfire. She kept bringing me coffee and killer homemade pizza to fuel that fire. You are the double eagle of wives.

Lastly, thank you to every reporter out there who keeps pursuing the truth head-first into the worst hurricane of lies, insults, and constitution-trampling I've seen in my 40 years in this business. You inspire me.

In a time of universal deceit, telling the truth is a revolutionary act.

—Unknown